Prosperity Magick

Prosperity Magick

Spells for Wealth

CASSANDRA EASON

AUTHOR OF *1001 SPELLS*

STERLING ETHOS
New York

STERLING ETHOS
New York

An Imprint of Sterling Publishing Co., Inc.
1166 Avenue of the Americas
New York, NY 10036

ISBN 978-1-4549-3678-7

Distributed in Canada by Sterling Publishing Co., Inc.
C/o Canadian Manda Group, 664 Annette Street
Toronto, Ontario M6S 2C8, Canada
Distributed in the United Kingdom by GMC Distribution Services
Castle Place, 166 High Street, Lewes, East Sussex BN7 1XU, England
Distributed in Australia by NewSouth Books
University of New South Wales, Sydney, NSW 2052, Australia

For information about custom editions,
special sales, and premium and corporate purchases,
please contact Sterling Special Sales at 800-805-5489
or specialsales@sterlingpublishing.com.

Manufactured in China

2 4 6 8 10 9 7 5 3 1

sterlingpublishing.com

Cover design by Elizabeth Mihaltse Lindy
Interior design by Sharon Jacobs

Image credits: Coin images: Bodor Tivadar/Shutterstock.com;
Other images © Sterling Publishing, Inc.

To my beloved family, Jade, Miranda, Tom, Jack, Bill, Freya, Holly, and Oliver, with special thanks to Kate Zimmermann, Konnie, and John Gold, who have all inspired and guided me.

Contents

Introduction

Prosperity Magick in Action

We all want financial security in our lives so that we can live without worry and fear, have a good home, travel, have enough to meet our needs (plus a little more), help those we love, and donate to the causes we deem most deserving of our support.

Money does not bring happiness in itself, and those who are obsessed with money rarely find contentment. But the spells in this book focus on the satisfaction of being rewarded for hard work and advancing toward a better quality of life. The book covers all aspects of prosperity, from building up security through savings, wise investments, or property, to gaining promotion and merited pay raises, to instant and urgent money for those times when we or our loved ones have a pressing need or we're overwhelmed by debt because of illness, misfortune, or the less-than-honest dealings of others.

Making money through our own creativity or enterprises can be especially satisfying, and building a business through our gifts, especially if there is fierce competition, can benefit from spells when starting out or in times of economic downturn. Spells can also help attract new business and expand markets and sources of income.

Turning an interest or hobby into a second or alternative career can benefit from a boost of magick. It can give us the confidence and impetus to test our talents in the marketplace, which these days often means cyberspace, and to attract the right publicity and consumers and build up a viable business. It can even help us achieve fame and fortune, should those be are dreams.

Money spells, like all magick, involve the dual process of drawing to us what we need when we most need it and alerting us to new opportunities through a natural psychic process called *psychokinesis*. Psychokinesis is the power whereby we spontaneously choose the right crystals to heal or the tarot cards to answer questions. In earlier times, it drew hunters to where the herds were when people had to travel on foot and did not have the resources of technological aids to guide them. Modern entrepreneurs seem to have this gift in abundance, but by casting prosperity spells frequently, we can all develop it to some degree.

When we hit periods of bad financial luck, or when it seems that whatever we touch turns to dust, we can lose confidence and become jittery and attract even more financial loss. Spells to replace bad luck with good have the dual purpose of not only removing lingering bad vibes but also of attracting opportunities for good fortune.

While the addiction of gambling can destroy solvency, there are indeed money spells to prevent this and other forms of addiction that drain family resources. Moderate gambling and speculation, whether on the financial markets or in property, are potential money spinners.

While the lottery is arguably largely a random process, spells may enable us to move the odds in our favor for at least moderate wins.

Saving through months and years, whether for a home, a dream, travel, or our family's future college fees, can benefit from spells by boosting free income. Spells can also psychically guide us and draw to us potentially wise investments. Spells can potentially assist us in buying property in the short and long term. Not only is this true for buying a new home, but also for adding sources of rental income, renovating properties for profitable resale, or tuning into and anticipating property market rises.

But if we are deprived of what is rightfully financially ours, whether through dishonesty (especially in the modern world as a result of internet or telephone scams) inheritance disputes, or unjust denial of compensation, earthly justice can feel slow or weighted against us. In such cases, spells can redress the balance, especially when a major organization or a particularly vicious or unjust adversary opposes us.

Financial drains, often from people who make us feel responsible or guilty if we don't subsidize them, can also benefit from the reversing power of spells. Earthly input can help protect us from emotional pressures or even psychological vampirism, which is when resources and energy are being drained equally. Divorce settlements can be particularly bitter, especially if one partner is using vulnerable children as a weapon, or if one partner feels totally steamrolled or manipulated or they cannot afford a good lawyer. Spells can help to redress the balance, not least by generating the power to fight back and creating an aura of victory that can outface a bullying ex-partner and expose lies.

Because of their nature, money spells utilize coins and jewelry, especially those made of gold or silver. These are considered natural symbols of prosperity. The lucky green symbolizes currency of any denomination, while rich and vibrant crystals such as the red or golden-gleaming tiger eye support hard-working people who desire to achieve success. Lucky green aventurine or amazonite is the stone of opportunity. If you put these all together, they are called the Gambler's Crystals. Sparkling yellow citrine is often called the Merchant's Stone and is associated with business ventures or promotion. The basil plant is traditionally used in money-growing spells, bamboo is used for money luck, and fragrances such as rose or sage are frequently linked with longer-term prosperity spells.

Money can also be a liberator, offering the means to travel and fulfill dreams. Sometimes downsizing or funding an eco-venture, while not bringing wealth beyond measure, can fall under the mantle of money magick to bring in sufficient funds to allow you to lead a fulfilling life.

But money can also be a weapon, used to control partners and families. Protective and empowering money spells may help to break the dreadful physical and emotional hold. For example, a family property or fortune going back generations can trap a newcomer who marries into the family. This newcomer may find themselves obligated to satisfy certain demands of the family or risk financial punishment.

This book spans the spectrum of human experience, from the earliest searches for prosperity through bartering and trade to modern financial dealings involving computers and cyberspace.

Money is essential to buying food, putting a roof over our heads, and helping us to care for ourselves and our families. We need it to entertain ourselves and to enjoy many of life's pleasures, not to mention the sense of security and safety it can provide. Many of us want the best for those we love, and we aren't afraid to work hard to support them.

Money spells can help with a variety of financial problems, from getting the two hundred dollars urgently needed to buy a new tire for the car, to achieving great wealth or fame as the CEO of a major company, to getting out of debt, to buying clothes for the kids, to starting a business of your dreams and becoming self-sufficient. Prosperity Magick stands proudly beside Love Magick, Protection Magick, and Healing Magick in providing spells to make life easier and to help you maximize your earning potential. With your newfound wealth, you'll be better equipped to meet your own personal goals while also helping those closest to you pursue theirs.

CHAPTER 1

Instant AND Urgent Money

When money is urgently needed and we've exhausted every means of getting it, it's natural to panic. In such moments, we wind up sending out all kinds of scattered energies that are counterproductive to drawing in money.

Instant and urgent money spells are an excellent way to focus the necessary energies to attract money speedily when needed. Often, you'll find that, in the days or weeks after casting these spells, the perfect amount of money shows up (no more, no less). You may find it hiding somewhere within your own web of personal finances, or it may come to you through an outstanding debt or bill that you'd given up hope on receiving.

The magick can be unexpected. After completing a spell, exploring alternatives and brainstorming about sources of income usually help keep the energies flowing.

Instant and urgent money spells are for emergencies and crises only. They're not really meant for when you're a bit short on cash, as they help bring about the energies needed to break through obstacles preventing you from immediately receiving funds.

The money may come to you in the form of a gift, a delayed payment, a chance to pick up an extra shift at work, or the idea to sell something you no longer need for a good price.

When You Need Money and It Can't Wait

YOU WILL NEED

A beeswax candle ✳ A coin (preferably a Chinese lucky
coin) pressed into the soft wax (pre-melted and the candle
blown out) about three-quarters of the way down

TIMING

When there is no time to spare

THE SPELL

* Light the candle. While gazing into the flame, say the following words
  nine times in rapid succession: *Five hundred dollars and ninety-nine
  cents* (or however much you need in your country's currency), *to get this
  fast is my intent, I spread this light, the money is sent, and all is right, end
  of fright.*

* At the end of the final chant, blow out the candle, clap your hands nine
  times, and call out the amount of money you need.

* If nothing has happened within twelve hours, repeat the spell. Then let
  the spell do its work.

For a Specific Sum of Money to Solve a Problem as Fast as Possible

YOU WILL NEED

A fast-burning red wax candle * Patchouli or rose
essential oil, diluted in olive oil, in a dish

TIMING

When the need is urgent

THE SPELL

* Over the dish of oil, write in the air the precise amount of
  money needed.

* At the base of the unlit candle, trace the same amount.

* Lightly dab the index finger of your dominant hand in the oil. Use this
  finger to trace the amount all over the sides of the candle (don't go near
  the wick).

* Rub the rest of the oil onto the candle. Start from the top of the candle
  and go halfway down, then go from the bottom of the candle to its
  midpoint.

* While lighting the candle say, *As this flame does burn, so shall my money
  luck turn*, [name amount] *shall come to me, and my problem* [name it if
  you wish] *is resolved instantly.*

* Let the candle burn.

If You're Receiving Final Notices About Your Debts

Three or four spices: ginger, cinnamon, allspice, sesame, curry, cardamom, pepper, chili, or turmeric ∗ A purse ∗ Seven gold- or silver-colored coins, any denomination

TIMING

When urgent

THE SPELL

∗ On day one, add each chosen spice and one coin to the purse, saying, *Gold and silver, I have none, into my life shall money* [name amount] *come by* [name date], *whether by luck or opportunity, I ask urgently that this shall be.*

∗ Close and shake the purse, speaking and shaking faster, then toss it in the air, catch it, and hold it in closed hands while saying the words slower and slower, until it feels natural to stop.

∗ Repeat the spell for seven days in total, adding a coin every day, even if the spell has already worked.

∗ Keep the purse with the final notice.

To Bring In a Windfall of Money When You Have a Cash Flow Crisis

You will need a pot of salt ∗ A pot of coins
∗ A spoon ∗ A yellow candle
∗ A piece of white paper

TIMING

Wednesday

THE SPELL

∗ Light the candlewhile saying, *Candle bright, bring this night, money bright, to my sight.*

∗ Spoon salt on to the paper while saying, *Money grow, money flow, speedily, that an end to the crisis soon shall be.*

∗ Add salt to the paper and put down a coin to start a circle around the salt, repeating the second set of words.

∗ Add more salt and coins alternately, until the coin circle is complete.

∗ Blow out the candle, gather the salt in the paper, and tip the salt under a running cold-water tap, saying, *Money flow, grow for me, rapid inflow shall there be.*

∗ Return the coins to the pot.

To Hasten Promised Money to Relieve a Temporary Financial Crisis

YOU WILL NEED

You will need a ceramic pot with a lid * Seven coins
* Seven dried bay leaves

TIMING

Eight consecutive days

THE SPELL

* Open the pot and surround it in coins and bay leaves, alternating between each.

* Drop the first coin you set into the pot, saying, *What is mine I call without delay, I can wait no longer, this I say, my need is now,* [Name], *keep your promise anyhow.*

* Drop one bay leaf into the pot while repeating the words louder and more firmly.

* Replace the lid.

* Each day for another six days, repeat the spell, adding a coin and bay leaf each day. Speak even louder and more firmly every time.

* On the eighth day, hold the closed pot and shake it, while yelling, *my need is now,* [Name], *send my money anyhow.*

* Contact the money source daily.

A Seven-Day Tealight Money Spell for a Fast Turnaround of Your Finances if You Are Stuck

YOU WILL NEED

Seven red tealights in a circle ✳ On small pieces of paper,
write down demands that need settling urgently,
piled in the center of the circle

TIMING

Seven consecutive days

THE SPELL

* Light the first tealight farthest away from you, saying, *Spell of increase, money grow, that by* [name essential date] *I shall know, my finances will be OK, and I can this bill mountain pay.*

* Blow out the tealight, saying, *Come from the East, North, South, or West, help in whatever way is best, I send light, to make all right.*

* Leave everything in place.

* Each subsequent day, light an extra tealight clockwise and repeat the spell.

* On day seven, when all the tealights are alight, leave them burning, saying, *I send this light to make all right, the bill mountain crumbles away, security is here to stay.*

Wishes for Money to Come into Your Life Soon

YOU WILL NEED

A copper-colored coin, a silver-colored coin, and a
gold-colored coin if possible * Any wishing well

TIMING

Early morning

THE SPELL

* Cast the copper coin into the well and make your wish silently, then add
  aloud, *Copper, silver, gold, I ask not for wealth untold, but enough for my
  needs and a little more, wishing well, into my life let money pour.*

* Do the same with the other two coins; silver next, then gold, repeating
  the words.

* Finally, gaze into the well, saying, *Enough for my needs and a little more,
  copper, silver, gold, wishing well, let my wish unfold.*

* Leave a small tribute, such as some flowers or a few crystals, near the
  well in thanks to the water essences.

A Three-Moon Phase Ritual to Bring the Opportunity to Earn Extra Money Within a Month

YOU WILL NEED

Three moonstones

TIMING

Outdoors, once during the waxing moon, once during the full moon, and once during the waning moon

THE SPELL

* On the night of the waxing moon, hold up the moonstones toward the moon in your open-cupped hands, saying, *Maiden Moon, increase shall there be, for you and me. Bring to me opportunity.*

* Set a moonstone where it will not be disturbed.

* On the full moon, repeat the spell with two moonstones, changing the words to, *Mother Moon, may it be your pleasure, to fill my hands with silver treasure.*

* Set one of the moonstones aside. Put it in a place where it won't be disturbed.

* On the waning moon, repeat the spell with the remaining moonstone, changing the words to, *Grandmother Moon, as your light fades away, take the obstacles that block my way.*

* Move all three moonstones to where they will be found as a gift.

A Triple Viking Calling for Money Urgently Needed from a Source on Which You Had Given Up

YOU WILL NEED

A fast-burning red candle ✳ A letter opener or any inscribing tool ✳ A pine incense stick ✳ A thin twig with the bark scraped off ✳ A permanent red ink marker

TIMING

Thursday sunset

THE SPELL

* On both sides of the unlit candle, inscribe the *Fehu* rune, the symbol of wealth.

* Light the candle and then light the incense from the candle.

* Draw eight *Fehu* runes around the candle in incense smoke, holding the incense like a smoke pen.

* Draw the *Fehu* symbol on the twig in marker, saying, *Three by three the power is raised, the path will open now in many ways.*

* Leave candle and incense to burn.

* Carry the twig in a small pouch as a talisman of good fortune.

For the Fast Sale of an Item or Service to Bring Money Quickly

YOU WILL NEED

Any three of chili, mustard seeds, ginger, allspice, or cinnamon ⋆ An iron pyrite crystal ⋆ A bowl ⋆ A red drawstring bag ⋆ A red candle

TIMING

Before advertising the item or service online

THE SPELL

* Light the candle, saying, *Sell fast* [name what you are selling/offering], *and profitably, that there will be a quick return for me.*

* Put each spice in turn into the bowl, swirl the bowl, and pass it five times clockwise around the candle quickly, repeating the words five times.

* Do the same for the pyrite.

* Close the bag and pass it quickly around the candle five times.

* Blow out the candle, saying, *The power is free, to sell profitably, as I count three, one, two, three, three, two, one, offers come.*

* Keep the bag near your computer as you advertise the item or service online.

To Make Money Last Until Payday

A toy spinning top ★ Small battery-powered candles
arranged in a row, one for each day left till payday

Every day from now till payday

* On day one, switch on all the candles and start the top spinning,
  repeating until it stops, *Spinning top, do not stop, day by day keep money-
  spinning, so I'll know that I am winning.*

* Start it spinning for a second time, saying, *Money makes the world go
  around and so enough will be found till payday.*

* Spin it a third time while saying both sets of words.

* On day two, light one less candle and repeat the spell.

* Each day, light one less candle, until you reach the day before payday,
  when there should be only one light left. End the spell on the final day
  by saying, *Tomorrow is payday, we made it all the way, Hurray!*

Calling on St. Expedite in a Financial Emergency

A red cloth on a table * A triangular formation
with a red candle at the top, a picture of St. Expedite
printed from the internet at the bottom right, and a glass of
water at the bottom left * A white candle and a green
candle arranged side by side in the center of the triangle
* A piece of brown paper and a red pen
* A red rose * A small homemade cake

TIMING

Wednesday evening

14

THE SPELL

* On the paper write, St. Expedite, who answers all emergencies, I ask that you hear my plea, St. Expedite bring help to me.

* Put the paper under the picture.

* Light all three candles—red, white, then green—while repeating the words.

* Add a red rose to the altar and a small homemade cake.

* Let the candles burn through.

* Next morning, scatter the rose petals outdoors and crumble the cake for the birds.

Seashell Money Wishes When You Are Running Out of Options

YOU WILL NEED

Any four of basil, sage, rose, rosemary, patchouli, thyme, or mint * A bowl * A yellow candle * An open double-sided seashell (oyster or clam shell) * Thin twine * A pearl

TIMING

Wednesday

THE SPELL

* Light the candle and add each herb to the bowl in turn, then swirl the bowl nine times clockwise while saying these words nine times, *I call to me money power, asking for what I seek this hour* [name your need].

* Put a little herb mix inside half of the seashell, add the pearl, and bind the two shell halves together tightly with the twine, saying, *I bind the money powers inside, asking that my fortunes turn with the tide.*

* Blow out the candle.

* After the spell, cast the tied shell into flowing water, preferably the ocean or a tidal river on the outgoing tide.

* Scatter any remaining herbs at the waterside.

Calling Bariel, Angel of Small Miracles, to Salvage Seemingly Impossible Finances

YOU WILL NEED

Small white tealights, set in a circle around
a central white larger candle

TIMING

Three consecutive days

THE SPELL

* Light the central candle, saying, *Bariel, angel of small miracles, all other roads have reached their end, I ask you now a small miracle to send.*

* From the central candle, light clockwise the ring of candles while repeating the words.

* Blow out the central candle, but let the candle ring burn.

* On day two, replace the burned ring of candles. Relight the central candle, then the candle ring, and repeat the spell.

* On day three, replace the burned candle ring again. Just as before, light all the candles, but this time say, *Three by three, Bariel, I ask it shall be, that with a small miracle, you will save me.*

* Leave all to burn through.

A Brass and Gold Spell to Rapidly Open a Previously Closed Source of Income

YOU WILL NEED

A small gold earring　＊　Twelve brass washers or discs, the kind used in plumbing　＊　A bowl covered in gold foil　＊　Seven frankincense incense cones

TIMING

Sunday noon

THE SPELL

＊ Place the brass washers in the bowl, saying, *Each day each week, an open door I seek, no more the way closed shall be* [name what is not open to you], *grant to me welcome entry.*

＊ Put the gold earring in the center of the bowl on top of the brass, saying, *All that glitters is not gold, but give me a chance* [name who is blocking you] *and you shall see, and you shall behold, my worth and total efficiency.*

＊ Leave the gold bowl in natural light.

＊ Each day for seven days, burn a frankincense cone next to the bowl.

CHAPTER 2

Spells FOR Generating Long–Term Prosperity

There is nothing wrong with seeking prosperity for ourselves because, if we are constantly worried about our long-term financial future, it can be hard to focus on spiritual matters and our dreams. Some seek wealth untold, while others only want enough to meet their needs (plus a little extra). The spells in this chapter are meant to help you achieve your own personal version of financial stability and success.

In return for the fruits of a long-term prosperity spell, it is good under the laws of cosmic exchange to help others—not necessarily in money terms, but by offering time or practical help.

The spells in this chapter focus on generating money over the months and years ahead. Most importantly, they're meant to help you maintain future financial stability. Through symbolic means, they encourage your assets to grow steadily over time, rather than in quick bursts or one-off infusions, which was the focus of the previous chapter. This chapter's spells include burying coins in the soil around a money plant (such as basil) or adding coins or seeds regularly to a money pot kept in a warm place. Such actions help to incubate your financial inflow. The numbers 3, 4, 7, and 9 are considered especially lucky for prosperity.

An All-Purpose Ritual to Draw Continuing Prosperity Over the Coming Weeks, Months, and Years

YOU WILL NEED

Sunflower seeds in a jar * A small, sealable glass container, like a kitchen storage jar * A blue candle

TIMING

Ongoing

THE SPELL

* Each morning, light the candle, take a handful of sunflower seeds, and shake them three times in your open-cupped hands, saying, *Three by three, grow prosperity, through weeks and months and over years, may money continuously in my life appear and never disappear.*

* Add the seeds to the jar.

* Leave the jar with the lid on where natural light will shine on it.

* Every day for the next six days, repeat the words and actions.

* On day eight, scatter the seeds from the container for the birds or in an unlovely place.

* Wait a week. After that, repeat the eight-day spell cycle whenever you wish.

Generating Lasting Prosperity with Fire

YOU WILL NEED

Six green play money notes ✶ A fireproof pot with
a lid, lined with sand or soil ✶ Three frankincense
or sandalwood incense cones on a dish

TIMING

Waxing moon

THE SPELL

* Light the incense cones and pass each play money note through the
  smoke, saying, *Money generate, do not wait, so through the years prosperity
  will accumulate.*

* In a safe place, burn the notes one at a time in the pot, repeating
  the words for each, and put on the lid.

* When the incense is burned through and cool, add the ash to the pot.

* Scatter the mixed ash to the winds while repeating these words six times,
  fly free, return as lasting prosperity to me.

Making a Prosperity Altar

A statue associated with money (placed in the center), for example a Buddha or the Chinese money toad/frog with a coin in its mouth ★ Six Chinese divination coins ★ Two red candles, one on either side of the statue ★ Two Dragon's Blood or frankincense incense sticks, placed to the side of each candle ★ A red envelope

TIMING

Thursdays

THE SPELL

* Light the candles, then light the incense.

* Blow softly into each candle and incense, saying, *I make my offering, that I will have always sufficient in everything.*

* Pass each coin through the incense smoke, then around each candle, putting each coin in the envelope.

* When all the coins are in the envelope, seal it and place it beneath the statue.

* Leave candles and incense to burn.

* Each week, repeat the candle and incense lighting. Pass the envelope through each incense stick smoke and around each candle.

A Dragon Viking Rune Ritual for Accumulating and Increasing Wealth

YOU WILL NEED

A model dragon or a picture of one downloaded from the internet ★ Three red candles in a triangle around the model dragon ★ Nine gold-colored coins ★ A gold-colored pot

TIMING

Three consecutive mornings

GEBO

THE SPELL

* On each unlit candle, draw the *Gebo* prosperity rune with the index finger of your dominant hand.

* Light each candle, saying, *I call to me the Dragon fire, that I release at my desire. Prosperity shall grow more and more, every day greater than before.*

* Make a triangle of three coins outside the candle circle, repeating the words.

* Blow out the candles.

* Repeat the spell for the next two days, adding three more coins to the pot each day and retracing the rune on the unlit candles.

* Place the pot and the dragon where natural light will shine on them.

A Lucky Toad/Frog Spell for Prosperity

A Chinese lucky toad/frog with a coin in its
mouth or any model frog with a gold-colored coin
beneath it * Twelve gold-colored coins * A patchouli,
peach, or frankincense incense stick * A dish of sand or soil

TIMING

Thursday

THE SPELL

* Surround the toad with a circle of twelve coins.

* Light the incense stick. While holding it, write the following phrase in incense smoke over the toad and coin circle seven times with increasing speed, PROSPERITY GROW, WEALTH SHOW, THAT LASTING FINANCIAL SECURITY I MAY KNOW.

* When you can write no faster, plunge the incense's lighted end into the sand and clap seven times over the toad, repeating the words slower and slower until it feels natural to stop.

* Keep the toad in the southeast corner of the room you use for finances, with the coins placed in a circle around the toad.

25

A Lantern Pathway for Lasting Prosperity

YOU WILL NEED

A string of solar, indoor/outdoor ornamental electric
lanterns, or a row of battery-powered candles

TIMING

After dark

THE SPELL

* Switch on your lanterns or battery candles, saying, *I light the pathway to prosperity, I open the door to successful Destiny. May money come easily and remain in my life lastingly.*

* Turn around in a circle nine times either beneath the lantern string or in front of the candles while stamping your feet and clapping louder with each circle. Repeat the words louder and more firmly as you turn.

* End with a loud clap and stamp on the final *lastingly* and switch off the lights.

* Repeat the whole spell nine times in rapid succession. On the final time, leave the lights burning for a few minutes and recite the words nine times more, then switch off the lights.

A Piggy Bank or Money Box Accumulation Ritual

A piggy bank or money box with a slot at
the top * A gold candle * A gold-colored coin

Wednesdays ongoing

* Light the candle where its light will shine on the piggy bank/money box.

* Toss the coin in open-cupped hands seven times, each time tossing it higher, saying for each throw, *Increased be prosperity, may my fortunes grow ever higher, for to wealth I do aspire, so I ask that it shall be.*

* With the final toss, catch the coin, shake it seven times in closed hands, and repeat the words quickly seven times.

* Put the coin in the piggy bank/money box.

* Leave the candle to burn.

* Repeat the spell weekly with a new candle and coin.

* When the box is full, give the money to charity, leaving one coin in the box for new spells.

27

Growing Gradual and Lasting Prosperity and Financial Stability

YOU WILL NEED

A basil plant in a pot of soil or a money plant, such as lucky bamboo ✳ A green candle ✳ Any four money crystals, such as jade, dendritic or tree agate, green aventurine, or moss agate, placed in front of the candle ✳ Four red ribbons

TIMING

Four consecutive waxing moon days

THE SPELL

✳ Light the candle so light falls on the plant, attaching the first ribbon to the plant, saying, *Candle glow, financial security grow, increasing stability show, that gradual prosperity I will know.*

✳ Pass both your hands slowly clockwise over the crystals, saying, *So I incubate, so increase, that prosperity in my life will grow and never cease.*

✳ Plant the first crystal in the soil and blow out the candle.

✳ Repeat the spell for three more days. Then on day four, leave the candle to burn through.

Growing a Money Tree for Acquiring Serious Wealth

YOU WILL NEED

An outdoor tree, such as a bay, a palm,
or an orange tree, or an indoor palm or a large
aloe vera plant * Six small gold bells * Six gold ribbons

TIMING

The crescent moon

THE SPELL

* Tie a ribbon through each bell with six knots and then affix them to the tree's branches or plant's leaves, saying as you hang each, *Offerings I bring, gold for gold, money tree, your wealth unfold.*

* Gently swing each bell from its ribbon in turn, so all are ringing, saying, *Gold for gold, wealth untold, may gold in my life I soon behold.*

* Water your plant regularly and ring the bells in turn, repeating for each, *Money tree, grow for me, wealth untold, that gold for gold I may soon behold.*

* On special occasions, attach gold solar or fairy lights to the growing tree/plant.

A Prosperity Bag to Keep Money Flowing into Your Life Throughout the Upcoming Months

YOU WILL NEED

A red drawstring bag or purse ⋆ A magnet
⋆ Twelve cloves ⋆ A dish of salt
⋆ Twelve long pins (if possible, tipped with pearls)

TIMING

Sunday early

THE SPELL

* Hold the magnet over each pin in turn, naming a month for each pin, saying, *January, February,* [name all the months in turn], *the whole year through, may my fortunes monthly renew.*

* As you collect each pin on the magnet, drop it into the bag.

* When all are in the bag, add twelve pinches of salt to the bag and then twelve cloves, saying for the salt and then the cloves, *Salt of wealth, cloves of abundance, increase bring, through twelve months and more, in everything.*

* Put the magnet in the bag, knotting the bag nine times.

* Keep the bag with your financial papers.

A Year and a Day Kelp and Whiskey Prosperity Jar

YOU WILL NEED

Dried kelp (available from health food stores) or a
piece of seaweed * A glass jar with a lid
* Whiskey of any quality

TIMING

The night before the full moon

THE SPELL

* Place the kelp or seaweed in the jar and hold it up to moonlight or,
  if cloudy, to the light of a silver candle. Say, *As the tides do inward flow,
  let wealth in my life daily grow, and for a year and day, let money stay,
  may it increase and not ebb away.*

* Add whiskey until the jar is about three-quarters full and covering
  the kelp.

* Seal the jar and shake it gently three times, repeating the words
  three times.

* Place the jar on a window ledge and replace the contents and spell
  after a year and a day.

A Seed Accumulation Ritual for Incubating Money

A tub of fenugreek, sunflower, cumin, or coriander seeds ★ A ceramic pot with a lid

TIMING

Crescent moon

THE SPELL

* Put a handful of seeds in the open pot, place your hands around the pot, and whisper into it, *Incubate, accumulate, as seeds take root and bring forth green shoots, let all my endeavors flourish, as Mother Earth new seeds does nourish.*

* Put on the lid and set the pot near the kitchen stove or another source of heat.

* Each day, add a sprinkling of seeds to the pot while repeating the words and actions.

* When the pot is full, bury a third of the seeds in soil, scatter a third into the air, and place the rest into flowing water. Be sure to leave a few seeds in the bottom of the pot.

* Repeat the spell whenever you have time, with new seeds.

A Celtic Tree Stave Ritual for Attracting Lasting Money for A Major Life Advancement

A twig, smoothed free of bark ✳ Red paint or a
permanent red marker pen ✳ Two small pieces of gold,
such as gold earrings ✳ A white cloth and red twine

TIMING

Sunrise or sunset

THE SPELL

33

* On the twig, paint or draw *Ngetal Ferns*, representing gold.

* When the paint is dry, wrap the twig in the cloth with the gold.

* Tie the top with twine in three knots, saying, *I call abundance in every
  way, I call prosperity in my life to stay, that I may make my big advance*
  [name if you wish], *ferns give me my golden chance.*

* Go to an open space, casting your bundle as far as you can into the
  bushes, saying, *Where this shall land, the old myths say, gold shall flow
  day by day.*

CHAPTER 3

Reversing Bad Luck IN Money, Money Losses, AND Encouraging Good Fortune IN Financial Affairs

Reversals in financial fortunes can happen for many reasons: a downturn in the economy, a sudden unpredictable collapse of a business or the loss of contracts on which we depend, an unwise decision, a redundancy or layoff, or the dishonest dealings of others.

Whatever the cause, we can lose our confidence and, like a psychic snowball, unconsciously attract further misfortune or miss opportunities through fear.

Spells for reversing bad luck are double focused, first to remove the ill fortune and then to replace it with good opportunities. This involves cutting or burying old ties to bad luck and symbolically regrowing new energies. Additionally, the spells generate extra confidence that in itself opens up your energies, both to attract better fortune and spontaneously guide you to where fresh opportunities lie.

A Tiger Eye Ritual for Restoring Prosperity After Major Loss

YOU WILL NEED

Two brown candles ✳ Two tiger eye crystals
✳ Two patchouli or sandalwood incense
sticks ✳ A brown drawstring bag

TIMING

Crescent moon and full moon

THE SPELL

* On the night of a crescent moon, light the candle and an incense stick.

* Draw a large dollar sign (or your local currency) over the first tiger eye in the air in incense smoke, saying, *Prosperity return once more, even greater than before, overcome loss, replace with gain, that my fortunes will rise again.*

* Put the tiger eye in the bag, close the bag, and knot it, then pass the bag around the candle three times clockwise.

* Leave the incense and candle to burn.

* Hang the bag in a high open place.

* On the night of the full moon, repeat the spell. Afterwards, open the bag, place the crystals on top, and leave them under the moonlight all night.

A Lucky Bamboo Ritual for Overcoming a Bad Financial Period That Seems to Never End

A lucky bamboo plant ⋆ A purple piece of string
⋆ A red ribbon ⋆ Scissors or a sharp knife

TIMING

Saturday

THE SPELL

* Tie the purple string with three loose knots around the bamboo, saying, *I wind and bind bad finances here, breaking the cycle of loss and fear.*

* Cut the string, saying, *I cut the power of loss without end, asking Dame Fortune prosperity to send.*

* Tie the ribbon in three loose bows around the bamboo where the string was, saying, *Bright luck, good fortune I bind financially, that my revival in fortunes shall lasting be.*

* Throw away the string and add a ribbon every week to the bamboo stem until no more will fit.

A Waxing Moon Ritual to Take Away a Run of Bad Financial Luck

YOU WILL NEED

A glass bowl, half filled with water
* Seven silver coins

TIMING

Three nights before the full moon

THE SPELL

* Drop the coins one after the other into the bowl, saying, *Lady Moon, wash away this financial misfortune from my life today.*

* Dip your hands in the water, rippling it.

* Next morning, set the coins in a plastic container with sufficient moon water to almost fill it.

* Put the container in the freezer untilthe night of the full moon.

* Take it out, let the ice melt, and pour the coins and water into the glass bowl.

* Under the moonlight, plunge your hands into the water and say, *Lady Moon, fill my hands with silver and gold, to gather all that I can hold.*

* Tip the water on the ground and spend the coins.

A Slow Regrowth Ritual to Rebuild a Past Financial Failure or Setback

YOU WILL NEED

A stone fruit, such as a plum, peach, or apricot,
turning brown ✳ A crossroads, or make
one with two crossed sticks

TIMING

The end of a week or month

THE SPELL

✳ Find soft earth at a crossroads or where you have created one and
dig a hole.

✳ Hold your fruit and say, *May misfortune from the past decay, and from it
growth come my way.*

✳ Place the fruit in the hole and cover it with earth, saying, *What cannot
be revived, will rise again, past efforts have not been in vain, I trust
⋯ ⋯ ⋯ for me it is not too late.*

⋯ ⋯ ng what did not work out.

A Lucky Buddha Return of Money if You Have Been Unjustly Deceived or Deprived of Resources

YOU WILL NEED

A wooden or metal laughing Buddha ✳ A small dish to place in front of the Buddha ✳ Necklaces, especially gold-colored ✳ Fresh yellow or gold flower heads

TIMING

Weekly on a Tuesday

THE SPELL

* Place a necklace around the neck of the Buddha and a fresh flower in the dish, saying, *I make my offering, asking wise Lord that you will bring, my good fortune, taken so unjustly, back to me.*

* Rub the tummy of the Buddha, firstly three times counterclockwise and then six times clockwise, saying, *May that of which I was unfairly deprived, be restored threefold and my good luck revived.*

* Each day replace the flower, and once a week, add another necklace. Repeat the second set of words as you complete these actions.

To Replace Ongoing Bad Financial Fortune with a New Lucky Money Break

YOU WILL NEED

A dark stone * A green aventurine or amazonite crystal
* A grey candle * A green candle
* A dish of soil

TIMING

Saturday

THE SPELL

* Put the dark stone in front of the grey candle and the aventurine in front of the green one.

* Light the grey candle. Holding the dark stone in your open hands, face the candle and say, *Within this stone passes misfortune and financial sorrow, that they will not rise on the morrow.*

* As you hold the stone, focus on what went wrong.

* Extinguish the candle, saying, *May misfortune be gone with the dimming of this light.*

* Bury the stone.

* Light the green candle and hold the green crystal lightly, saying, *Opportunity will I take, to offer my financial break.*

* Leave the candle to burn. Carry the green crystal as a charm.

To Remove the Lingering Effects of a Bad Financial Decision or Break and Bring New Input

YOU WILL NEED

Two pieces of white paper * Water-soluble red ink
* A small, flat container filled with water
* Scissors * A gold glitter pen

TIMING

Sunrise

THE SPELL

* Write on the first piece of paper in red ink, THIS IS THE SUM OF MY LOSSES [write approximate amount]. I DISSOLVE THEM CLEAN AWAY, FROM BLIGHTING MY LIFE, THEY MAY NO LONGER STAY.

* Cut the paper into pieces and press them into the container of water until it is covered.

* Leave the paper in the water till the water turns red.

* Then place the container with paper and water into the freezer.

* On the second piece of paper, in gold pen, write, BRIGHT FORTUNE, SHIMMER WITH NEW LIGHT, BRING FRESH HOPE INTO SIGHT.

* Hang the paper where the noon light will shine on it every day.

An Olive Ritual for When Financial Luck Has Dried Up

YOU WILL NEED

A small bowl of olive oil ★ A dishful of golden-green
olives with pits ★ A small, lidded pot for the pits

TIMING

Thursday morning

THE SPELL

* Slowly pour the olive oil away under running water, saying, *Drained away, diluted day by day, but without fear I let the old flow away.*

* Let the diluted olive oil run away until the bowl is empty.

* Set the bowl of olives in the center of the kitchen table and eat a few, saying, *I take in sweet prosperity, that good fortune once more will enter me.*

* Put the pits in the lidded pot, and when you have eaten all the olives, over the following few days, bury all the pits, saying, *Ripen slow, unfold the growing gold, for I do know, the stones inside, ever-increasing opportunities hide.*

Recalling Money Luck into Your Life if You Seem to Have Gradually Lost It

Any green currency note * Six silver coins for luck
* Sticky tape

TIMING

The day before a full moon

THE SPELL

* Place the coins on the note, which should be just in front of you.

* Hold your fingers over the coins and move your hands about half an inch above them towards you as if beckoning them, saying, *Come back to me, flow back easily, reverse the trend, that money rolls towards me without end.*

* Touch each coin in turn and start to roll the note towards you, enclosing the coins within it, repeating the words continuously.

* Finally, tuck the ends of the note to make a parcel and secure with a little sticky tape.

* Keep the note in a wallet or money purse.

45

A Hair Ritual for Binding in Financial Fortune

YOU WILL NEED

Eight hairs from your head ★ A silver or gold ring
★ A silver chain ★ Red thread

TIMING

Saturday sunset

THE SPELL

* Bind the hairs around the ring, using thread to attach them. Say,
*I bind my strength, I wind my strength, I tie good fortune in, money is
held, good luck is safe, secure and firm within.*

* Attach the ring to the chain and suspend it at a window for a full
seven-day cycle so that light will pour into it.

* Then wear the ring around your neck out of sight for a further seven
days. During this time, say the words, *I wind my strength, I bind my
strength, I fill it with my heart, from this day good things shall stay and
bring a brand new start.*

* After seven days, return the ring to the window to act as a
money magnet.

A Lemon Pig Ritual from Chile for Taking Away Financial Misfortune and Attracting Major Good Fortune

YOU WILL NEED

A lemon ✶ Shiny pins ✶ A shiny magnet ✶ A very deep bowl of salt

TIMING

Wednesday

THE SPELL

* Stick four pins into the lemon to act as legs for the pig.

* If you wish, draw features and a curly tail.

* Scatter the remaining pins around the pig in a circle, saying, *Lemon pig, I ask this day, you take financial sorrow away.*

* Put the pig upside down in the bowl of salt so only the legs stick out.

* Using the magnet, pick up the circle of pins clockwise, saying, *Draw to me good fortune, advantage, and prosperity.*

* Place the magnet with the pins still attached where the first morning light will catch it each day.

* When the pig has dried and shrivelled, take out the pin legs, wash them, attach them to the magnet, and bury the lemon.

An Elephant and Mouse Luck Growing Ritual

YOU WILL NEED

A small ceramic mouse
★ Three model elephants in ascending size

TIMING

Sunset, sunrise, and noon

THE SPELL

* At sunset, set the mouse outside the front door, saying, *I need not fear the misfortune mouse, no longer shall s/he remain in my house.*

* Put the smallest elephant on the bottom step of the stairs indoors or on a low surface, saying, *Unfettered, prosperity will rise, gone loss, gone fear, success is near, rising to the skies.*

* At sunrise, put the second-sized elephant halfway up the stairs or on a progressively higher surface than the first. Repeat the second set of spell words.

* At noon, put the largest elephant on the top step or an even higher surface than the second. Repeat the second set of words, then immediately remove the mouse from the premises.

A Money Spell if You Feel Whatever You Do Results in Financial Disaster

YOU WILL NEED

A purple cord * A small box * A small
padlock and chain * A white cord

TIMING

The day before the crescent moon

THE SPELL

* Tie a knot in the center of the purple cord, saying, *This knot I make, bad fortune I break, sorrow forsake.*

* Tie a second knot on top of the first and repeat the words.

* Do the same as you tie a third knot. Tie the two ends of the cord together, saying the same words.

* Place the knotted cord inside the box, secured with the padlock and chain.

* Tie a single knot in the white cord, saying, *I bind, I wind, I find, within this knot, all is right, incoming money and fortune held tight.*

* Hang the white cord on the inside your front door to filter out misfortune.

49

Increasing Prosperity Through Employment, Especially BY Promotion OR A New, Better Job

Work is one of the major ways most of us can increase our prosperity. Whether we're moving up the ladder of an existing career or embarking on an entirely new work path, spells can help us shine at interviews and get the promotions and pay raises we deserve.

Spells can also ensure that we have a fair chance at being rewarded through our abilities in the workplace. This way, advancement isn't solely determined by favoritism or internal politics.

Through study and training, new opportunities can arise. This can lead to improved job satisfaction or an advancement in your finances. Unfortunatly, it's not always easy if you're constantly working or have a busy life.

You can also find that promotion is blocked, not because of lack of ability, but because of internal politics or because you are taken for granted or overlooked. Often, a ritual will increase your profile so that you are noticed favorably and given the monetary rewards that are merited.

Finally, if we have suffered a layoff, spells can open new doors for us, no matter our age. They can illuminate new opportunities and help us overcome prejudices such as ageism or sexism. Best of all, they help us regain our confidence, even if our many job applications haven't proven successful so far.

To Perform Well in an Interview for a Major Pay Increase or New Job

YOU WILL NEED

Seven dried bay leaves, the kind you use for cooking
* A bowl of salt * A letter opener or long, sharp pin

TIMING

Seven consecutive days before the interview

THE SPELL

* On a bay leaf, scratch the following words with the sharp letter opener or pin: *May I make an impression, to open the door, that what I earn will become even more.* It does not matter if the words are hard to see.

* Dip the leaf briefly in the salt, saying the words out loud.

* Release the bay leaf outdoors, saying, *Fly today, show the way, to recognition and higher pay.*

* Do this every day for seven days.

* On the morning of the interview, tip the remaining salt under a running tap, saying, *May my interview please, may my salary increase, and advancement not cease.*

To Succeed in a Test, Interview, or Examination to Take You to the Next Pay Level

YOU WILL NEED

A red or brown tiger eye, a grey hematite, and a yellow citrine
★ A brown drawstring bag or purse

TIMING

The morning of the test, interview, or examination

THE SPELL

* Hold the tiger eye in your open-cupped hands.

* Shake it three times, saying, *I take my power, I shake my power, I will succeed, and the next pay level shall be mine indeed.*

* Add the hematite and shake both crystals three times while repeating the words.

* Finally, add the citrine to your hands and shake all three crystals three times while saying, *Three by three, the next pay level shall come to me.*

* Add the crystals to the bag.

* Take the bag to the test or interview. Before it begins, shake it three times while saying the words.

To Make a Financially Advantageous Move Within Your Present Organization

A tablespoon of dried powdered cinnamon
* A tablespoon of allspice * A tablespoon of
ginger * A tablespoon of unscented baby powder
or corn starch * Pine, rose, or lemongrass fragrance
oil * A bowl and spoon * A padded bag

TIMING

The evening before applying/the interview for the move

THE SPELL

55

* Add each herb in turn to the bowl, saying, *A move I seek within this company, to bring more opportunity and lots more money, over months and over years, the path to prosperity slowly appears.*

* Add a few drops of oil.

* Stir clockwise, repeating the words faster, then slow your movements and words until they fade.

* Place the mix in the paper bag.

* Before work, sprinkle a little of the mix near the front entrance and repeat the words.

* When you leave, scatter any remaining mix outside the building.

If You Are Always Passed Over for a Salary Increase and/or Promotion

YOU WILL NEED

Five gold bells
★ Five lengths of green cord

TIMING

Tuesday

THE SPELL

* Tie a knot at the top of the first cord, attach the first bell to it halfway down, and knot the bottom of the cord to the top of the second one, until all five bells are attached and all five cords are joined together.

* End with a knot at the bottom of the fifth cord.

* As you make each knot, say, *Notice me positively, reward me fairly, for my endeavors, that I may ever continue to increase my salary and due recognition see.*

* Hang the cord on the back of your front door.

* On the day you intend to tackle the matter, take the cord to work, touching each knot and ringing each bell subtly while repeating the words in your mind.

To Get a Well-Paid Job if You Have Lost Yours Through Layoff, Workplace Closure, or Illness

YOU WILL NEED

A grey, a dark blue, and a bright blue candle
* Olive oil in a dish

TIMING

Thursday

THE SPELL

* Rub the unlit grey candle with oil from the bottom to the center and from the top to the center, avoiding oil around the wick.

* Say, *Bring back the light, that I might get a new job, well paid, interesting and in every way fulfilling.*

* Repeat the same actions and words for the dark blue candle, first extinguishing the grey candle.

* Repeat for the bright blue candle, afterward extinguishing the dark blue candle.

* Relight the dark blue candle from the bright blue candle and the grey candle from the dark blue candle while saying the same words.

* Blow out all three candles fast, relight them—grey to dark blue to bright blue—and leave them to burn.

A St. Joseph Employment Blessing for Turning a Temporary Job into a Better-Paid Permanent One

YOU WILL NEED

A natural beeswax candle ★ White paper and an envelope ★ A blue pen ★ Dried sage

TIMING

Seven nights

THE SPELL

* Light the candle and write on the paper, GOOD ST. JOSEPH, GUARDIAN OF ALL WHO FOR THEIR LIVING STRIVE, GRANT ME PERMANENT WORK THAT I MAY THRIVE AND SECURE BE FINANCIALLY, I WILL WORK HARD IF YOU GRANT THIS TO ME.

* Put the folded paper in the envelope with a pinch of sage.

* Blow out the candle.

* Repeat daily, leaving the paper in the envelope in front of the candle. Add a pinch of sage before blowing out the candle.

* On day seven, after adding the last pinch of sage, drip a little wax on the envelope to seal it.

* Leave the candle to burn through. Keep the envelope with your applications.

To Overcome Fierce Competition if You Are Striving for a Well-Paid Job with Good Future Prospects

YOU WILL NEED

A dish of mixed salt, pepper, and sugar
* Tibetan bells * A small silver purse

TIMING

The evening before the interview/application

THE SPELL

* Every hour for four hours, ring the bells over the mix as you say, four times, *Bells, I call upon your power, to stand for me at every hour, competition to overcome, that prosperity through this new job will come.*

* After the fourth hours' ringing, add four pinches of the mix to the purse and repeat the words four more times.

* Close the purse.

* Next morning, add four more pinches to the purse and ring the bells four times over the mix while repeating the words four times.

* Take the purse with you to the interview or when making the application. Afterwards, wash the mix away.

To Be Accepted into a Long-Term Training Program That Will Give You a Secure and Prosperous Career

YOU WILL NEED

Two golden candles and seven small white tealights set as a diagonal pathway between them ∗ Seven small yellow citrine

TIMING

Any appropriate time during the application/selection process

THE SPELL

∗ Light the golden candle nearest to you.

∗ Blow softly into the flame, saying, *I light the pathway to a golden future for me for success, fulfilment, and prosperity, step-by-step and stage-by-stage, I seize this road with hope and courage.*

∗ Light each of the tealights in turn, setting a citrine in front of each and repeating the words.

∗ Finally, light the second golden candle and say the words again.

∗ Leave all to burn through.

∗ Keep the citrine in a circle around any written communication/your computer, touching each crystal and repeating the words before each major step.

To Earn Big Money if There is a Glass Ceiling in the Way of Advancement

YOU WILL NEED

A small glass lidded jar ★ Twelve small clear quartz crystals or glass nuggets ★ A silver candle ★ A glass bowl half filled with water

TIMING

The night of a full moon

THE SPELL

* Before the full moon rises, light the candle next to the jar. Add the crystals/nuggets to the jar and put the lid on.

* Say, *Reflected light, reflected glory, this no longer shall be my story.*

* Take off the lid.

* Drop the crystals/nuggets into the bowl of water, saying, *The glass ceiling is gone, restrictions are done, I reach for opportunity and so money shall flow to me and success be won.*

* Leave the bowl outdoors. Next morning, put the crystals in the jar without the lid.

* Bottle the moon water to splash on pulse points in the days ahead whenever you experience doubt.

To Ask for a Long-Overdue Promotion or a Salary Raise if You Are Being Taken for Granted

YOU WILL NEED

A mirror ⋆ A favorite piece of gold
or crystal jewelry

TIMING

Bright sunlight shining in the mirror

THE SPELL

* Put on the jewelry and touch it. Look into the mirror and say,
  *May I shine bright as the sun, what I deserve shall be won, away goes fear,
  away goes doubt, the answer "no" I do cast out.*

* Turn away from the mirror and shake your hands away from you.

* Turn back, face the mirror again, touch the jewelry once more, and say,
  *Within this, is the answer "yes, " a raise and promotion, I shall receive no
  less, I shine bright as the sun, my request is won.*

* When you are ready to make your request for promotion/a raise, touch
  the jewelry and ask with confidence.

If You Are Losing Hope of Finding a Well-Paid Job in an Overcrowded or Declining Market

YOU WILL NEED

A bag full of small, dark-colored stones ⋆ A larger
pure white stone or crystal, also placed in the bag

TIMING

The day before the full moon

THE SPELL

* Shake the bag of stones nine times while saying these words nine times,
  Far too many, seeking the prize, from the crowd I need to rise.

* Open the bag and remove the white stone. Hold it and say, *From the
  crowd do I stand out, noticed favorably I shall be, of all the rest, I am the
  best, and so the right job and right salary, shall come to me.*

* Tip the dark stones out the front door and carry your white stone in the
  bag as a talisman. Place it on top of any applications or interview offers.

Overcoming Ageism, Sexism, or Favoritism if You Are Being Denied Advancement

YOU WILL NEED

A sealed tube of children's bubbles with a blower
* A long gray thread knotted around the
bubble tube * A sharp knife

TIMING

Sunday

THE SPELL

* Hold the tangled jar, saying, *All my gifts, all my skills, bound by prejudice, false favors and ill will* [name the particular prejudice that blocks you].

* Cut through the threads with the knife, saying, *No longer shall my talents hide, I will reveal the talents blocked inside. Advance I will so much more, no longer shall prejudice bar my door.*

* Go outdoors and blow the bubbles into the air, saying, *Fly high, fly free, financial advantage shall come to me, no more shall hidden obstacles binding be. My efforts now rewards shall see.*

* When the bubble blower is empty, compose your e-mail or plan your approach to knock down those barriers.

To Obtain Good Bonuses, Perks, and Incentive Payments

YOU WILL NEED

A gold candle * A big, gold-colored dish
* Golden coins and notes of different
denominations * Any old jewelry

TIMING

Daily for a week

THE SPELL

* Each day light the candle so that it shines on the dish. Add treasures from your collection and say, *May money accumulate, bonuses, perks, payments, grow, that financial incentives I shall know.*

* Shake the dish three times and say the following words three times, *Accumulate, that rewards will become progressively greater.*

* Blow out the candle fast.

* By day seven, the dish should contain all the treasures. Leave the candle to burn.

* Keep the dish where morning light will shine on it.

* Every seven days, light a new candle, add a new item of jewelry, shake the dish three times, and repeat the following words three times, *Accumulate, that rewards will become progressively greater.* Leave the candle to burn.

* Continue until the bowl is full.

CHAPTER 5

Making Your Own Money Through Self-Employment

tarting or running your own business is one of the most satisfying ways of earning a living. Of course, there can be drawbacks, including not getting a regular, guaranteed salary, not getting paid holidays, and not going home at a set time, which are often the benefits of working for others. But many would argue that having the flexibility and autonomy of steering your own ship far outweighs the disadvantages of being your own boss.

This chapter is intended to help with every aspect of attaining success and satisfaction in self-employment. There are spells for starting a business, building up contacts during the early days of your new venture, overcoming setbacks and economic downturns, protecting your business from dishonesty, jealousy, and unfair competition, and attracting extra business when things are slow. Spells can also help you turn talents, hobbies, and interests into new businesses or transform good ideas into profitable sources of income. Later chapters focus on the attainment of fame and fortune, but for many of us, simply being able to earn a living through our own gifts and talents is reward enough.

To Generate Success and Initiative in Your Business if You or Other Workers Are Lacking Enthusiasm

YOU WILL NEED

A small clear crystal sphere or clear glass paperweight
set near the center of your business workplace

TIMING

The brightest part of the day

THE SPELL

* Hold the sphere between cupped hands so that light fills it. Say,
  *Fill my business with vitality, flood it with prosperity, let this light through
  all things shine, crystal sphere make success mine.*

* Lift the crystal so it further catches the light, then carry it raised in
  both hands throughout your workspace and say, *Light shine, enthusiasm
  radiate, every aspect permeate, crystal sphere make success mine.*

* Return the sphere to the center of the workspace and wash it under
  running water, repeating the spell weekly.

To Launch or Expand a Creative Business

Seven small silver candles in a circle
★ An incense stick in myrrh or jasmine

TIMING

Monday, day of the moon, for seven consecutive days

THE SPELL

* Light the candle farthest away, saying, *Lady of the Moon, Monday and every day, launch/expand my creative business soon 0* [describe it].

* Continue to light candles until all are alight.

* Hold the incense stick in each candle in turn. In the air over the lighted candle circle, write in incense smoke and say, *May my creativity bring prosperity, to my new/expanding business soon. Monday and every day, Lady of the Moon.*

* Blow out the candle and leave the incense burning.

* Repeat the spell every day, changing the first chant to, [name the appropriate day] *and every day*.

* On day seven, leave the candles burning.

A Sun and Moon Ritual to Attract Customers in Person and Via the Internet into Your Business

YOU WILL NEED

A jar of dried sage, mint, and basil
* A bowl and spoon * Cornstarch or unscented baby powder * A waterproof bag

TIMING

Any afternoon between the crescent and full moon, when sun and moon are in the sky at the same time

THE SPELL

* Add a tablespoon of each herb and cornstarch to the bowl, then, while swirling the bowl nine times clockwise, say, *Herbs of prosperity, draw to me, customers to my business that I will see, a fast and lasting upswing in everything.*

* Tip the contents into the bag and leave it for a few hours to absorb joint sun and moon energies.

* The following morning, sprinkle a little herb mix outside the main entrance or door to your workplace.

* Do this daily until the mix is all used.

A Nine-Day Knot Spell for Launching a Solo Business or Rapidly Expanding an Existing One

YOU WILL NEED

A long yellow cord or ribbon ★ A yellow candle ★ A bowl of salt

TIMING

Wednesday

THE SPELL

* Light the candle.

* Hold the cord so you singe the ends. Then say, *Flame and flare, fire alive, release the power, that my new/existing business may thrive.*

* Sprinkle salt at each end of the cord, saying, *Power of the Earth, come alive, release the power, that my new/existing business may gain drive.*

* Tie nine knots, top to bottom, saying both chants for each knot.

* Leave the knotted cord in front of the candle till the candle is burned.

* Hang the knot on the inside of the front door of your business, undoing a knot every day beginning the morning after the spell.

* After the knots are undone, repeat the spell if you wish.

To Cleanse Your Business Premises of All Negative and Stuck Energies if You Are Taking Over a Failed Premises or There Have Been Previous Problems

YOU WILL NEED

Three small round amethysts * Three small pointed clear quartz crystals * A green plant, such as mint or basil * Two small bowls of water

TIMING

Daily

THE SPELL

* Soak the amethysts in one bowl and the quartz in the other, setting them in front of the plant in the center of your business premises.

* Each morning sprinkle the doorsteps and thresholds of room/s and the plant with first the amethyst water, then the quartz water. Then say, *Clear all negativity and unhelpful forces that drain away energy, heal this place, with positivity replace, that to these premises abundance shall return.*

* Tip away remaining water on workplace plants at the end of the day.

* Refill the bowls, adding the crystals before leaving work.

To Restore Money and Customer-Attracting Energies

YOU WILL NEED

Dust from near an old ant or termite hill
★ Coriander and cumin seeds ★ Any green
crystal, such as aventurine ★ A pot filled with
soil collected near your business premises

TIMING

The first day of your working week

THE SPELL

* Mix the soil with the termite hill dust well, saying, *Ants/termites constantly you strive, give me likewise persistence and effort that my business will thrive.*

* On top of the soil in the pot, make a rough spiral shape with the seeds.

* Place the crystal in the center, saying, *Draw back, restore once more, money hold fast, bring customers that new success will last.*

* Bury the seeds and crystal within the pot and add a thriving green plant to it, then place the potted plant near the center of the workplace.

For a Constant Inflow of Orders and Payments for Goods or Services Through a Conventional or Internet Business

A printout of a recent currency note taken or the most recent electronic or credit card payment made to you
* A yellow citrine crystal, the Merchant's crystal
* Sticky tape

TIMING

Before shutting down for the night

THE SPELL

* Place the citrine on the printout, then toss the citrine progressively higher five times, saying, *Money, orders pouring through the door, increasing daily more and more.*

* Catch the crystal on throw five.

* Returning the citrine to the printout, roll the sides of the printout and top and bottom to make a parcel.

* Seal it with tape, saying, *Hold fast my endeavor, keep it safe and sure, so increasing input shall increase and endure.*

* Keep the parcel where you take in money (the actual space or the room where you accept it electronically).

* Replace the parcel after a year and a day.

Casting Fortune Before You

A coin in each denomination from the lowest
to the highest in your local currency

TIMING

*Every morning before entering your business premises/
workspace, until you have used all the coins*

THE SPELL

* Stand outside the door and face inwards.

* Throw a coin so it lands in the doorway. Then say, *May money follow, from lowest to the high, may my success keep soaring to the sky.*

* Put the coin somewhere above the door. Coins should be placed left to right in rising value or in a high place.

* Repeat the spell each day with a coin of increasing value until you have used all your coins. You can also do this when moving into a new home or business premises.

To Bring Lasting Good Luck to Your Business

Nine Chinese divination coins with holes in the center
* A long red cord or ribbon * A square lucky candle
with a Chinese coin in it or a pre-softened beeswax
candle with a Chinese coin inserted into the wax

TIMING

Waxing moon

THE SPELL

* Shake the loose coins in your open-cupped hands nine times, saying, *Lucky, lucky, luckier shall I be, luck shall come from far and wide, over land and sea.*

* After lighting the candle, repeat the words nine times.

* Knot each of the coins at regular intervals. Say the words nine more times for each knot.

* Leave the cord lying in front of the candle until the coin is free from the candle.

* Attach this last coin still with wax on it to the cord and knot the bottom of the cord.

* Hang it near a window.

Stirring Energies in an Economic Downturn or Fierce Business Competition

YOU WILL NEED

A wind chime ∗ A small candle on a plate
∗ A bowl of water with a white flower head floating

TIMING

Sunday

THE SPELL

∗ Walk around the room/business premises from outside the front door facing inwards and ring your wind chime clockwise while continuously saying, *Stir the energies within, free from worry shall this week begin, on a high note also end, success and prosperity inward send.*

∗ Light the candle. Walk around the whole room/premises again while repeating the words.

∗ Then sprinkle the water clockwise around the whole premises.

∗ Leave the candle to burn. The flower water should be left in the center of the main area until the flower fades.

∗ Hang the wind chime inside the front door and daily ring it at the start of the day.

A Rune Ritual for When You Fear You May Lose Your Business

The Uruz rune, rune of the Aurochs, the huge
Wild Oxen * A children's chalkboard
* White chalk * Water

TIMING

Saturday at sunset

THE SPELL

* All over the chalkboard, write the words, I SHALL NOT FALL, I SHALL NOT
  FAIL, IN SPITE OF ALL OBSTACLES I MUST PREVAIL, I SHALL SURVIVE, BY
  THE POWER OF THE WILD OXEN, I WILL THRIVE.

* Put the board flat on the ground and pour water over it
  until the words disappear. Say, *Fortune reappear, bright and clear,
  by the power of the Wild Oxen, I shall not fear.*

* If there is any smearing, clear the board with a cloth. When the board
  is dry, fill the board with a large Uruz sign.

* Keep this where you can see it. If the chalk image fades, touch it up.

To Turn an Interest or Talent into a Profitable Business

YOU WILL NEED

A sample/symbol of your venture ★ Six silver
coins or thin silver rings/earrings

TIMING

Crescent moon and full moon

THE SPELL

* On the crescent moon, raise first your symbol/sample in the direction of the crescent in the hand with which you write. Hold the six coins in the other open hand.

* Raise the symbol and the coins alternately, six times in total, and say the following words six times, *Crescent Moon as you do grow, let my venture likewise so.*

* Surround the symbol with the coins. Leave it in a sheltered place all night.

* Repeat on the full moon, saying, *Mother Moon in your full power, I ask success on me you shower.*

* Finally, cast each coin as far as you can and say, *By the time the moon is new, make my venture flourish too.*

A Celtic Tree Stave Ritual to Grow a Business from a Small but Viable Idea

YOU WILL NEED

A smooth stick or twig ✳ A red permanent marker pen or red paint and a thin brush ✳ An acorn, apple seeds, or pits from a fruit

TIMING

Early in the morning

THE SPELL

✳ On the stick, paint the Ido/Yew Tree stave to represent gradual but permanent growth.

✳ When you have finished, say, *Yew tree, you bring to me, growth from this seed, through months and years, a secure career comes ever near.*

✳ Plant your acorn or fruit pit and say, *Mighty oaks from tiny acorns grow, with perseverance and patience, I do know, this venture will likewise stand tall, I venture and so I shall win all.*

✳ Place your tree stave on top to mark the place of planting and do something to help start your venture, even if it's only a small step.

To Deter Jealous Rivals or Industrial Sabotage

YOU WILL NEED

Two Dragon's Blood incense sticks ★ Your business
card placed between the incense sticks ★ Salt and
pepper in a pot ★ An old broom or brush

TIMING

Before you open for business at the beginning of the week

THE SPELL

* Holding a lighted incense stick in each hand, spiral the active hand
  incense clockwise and the other counterclockwise while continuously
  saying, *Keep from my business all jealousy, drive away unfair opposition,
  banish all bad-intentioned competition, that sabotaging shall cease to be.*

* Return the incense to their holders.

* When they are burned, add the cooled ash to the salt and pepper pot.

* Scatter the mix on the doorstep of your business.

* With the broom, sweep it outwardand say, *Old broom, take from me all
  negativity that against my business there is and shall be.*

* Dispose of the broom.

To Attract Good Custom and Deter Thieves, Non-Paying Customers, and Troublemakers

YOU WILL NEED

Eight quartz crystals pointed at one end * Eight obsidian arrows or pointed black tourmaline crystals

TIMING

The beginning of a month

THE SPELL

* Set two obsidian arrows (pointing outward) on opposite sides of the front/main workspace door while saying, *Barred and banished shall you be, all who approach with ill intent, from this moment onwards, your malice is finished and spent.*

* Put the remaining dark crystals in pairs on opposite sides of any vulnerable space. Make sure they are pointed outward toward the main door.

* Set two clear points inside the dark ones, facing inwards, either side of the front door, saying, *Welcome all with good intent, enter by the score, prosperity shall be drawn in, profit increase more and more.*

* Do the same for the remaining clear ones, pointing inwards, always just inside each dark crystal.

CHAPTER 6

Attracting Prosperity AND Abundance IN THE Home AND Garden

For centuries, people have used spells and magical bags in hopes of gaining more food, clothing, and other essentials to allow their families to survive another year. The spells in this chapter are meant to boost domestic prosperity. They're centered on actual foodstuffs and objects commonly found in the kitchen.

Domestic prosperity spells often involve incubating or growing good fortune. They focus on tried and tested magick from different traditions across the world and have been adapted to fit the 21st century. Such magick normally makes use of lucky tokens such as coins, plants, and fragrances.

Domestic prosperity spells gradually draw money, resources, and financial opportunities into the home and prevent wealth from draining away. What was traditionally the family hearth, now the center or heart of the home, is the place to which prosperity and abundance can be gathered, held safe, and circulated throughout the home and to all its members. Balconies and gardens (both indoor and outdoor) can also be used to draw in wealth. The greatest advantage of domestic magick is that it also naturally carries protective and health-improving powers, which can benefit your life beyond just your finances.

To Activate Dragon Prosperity to Flow Through Your Home

YOU WILL NEED

A model dragon, either green, red, or gold, ideally metal ✳ A string of prayer flags or party streamers ✳ A permanent gold marker

TIMING

Noon

THE SPELL

✳ On the back of each prayer flag or individual streamer write, in gold, MAY THE PROSPERITY OF THIS HOME ALWAYS FLY HIGH.

✳ Emphasize the dragon's eyes by painting them gold, saying, *May good fortune shine bright and clear, may prosperity enter and never leave here.*

✳ Hang the prayer flags message inwards across the highest place in your home and repeat these words, *May the prosperity of this home always fly high.*

✳ Set your dragon where you handle your finances (make it face east). You can also place it in the southeast part of your home.

✳ Whenever you have a money outflow, retouch the dragon eyes with gold and repeat these words, *May good fortune shine bright and clear, may prosperity enter and never leave here.*

To Ensure Wealth Enters Your Home and Never Leaves

YOU WILL NEED

One of each coin of ascending value in your local currency ⋆ Gold sticky tape ⋆ The doormat outside your front door ⋆ A gold candle

TIMING

Crescent moon

THE SPELL

* Outdoors, hold the coins upwards to the moon in open-cupped hands, saying, *As the moon increases, so shall money grow, leading inwards, never outward, soon shall fortunes flow.*

* Go indoors and light the candle. Hold the coins to the light while repeating the words.

* Tape the coins diagonally across the underside of the mat, smallest to largest, so when the mat is on the doorstep the right way up, they form a pathway inwards.

* Say, as you place the mat, *Low to high, so fortunes rise, within does come wealth as all pass in.*

* Every time you enter, stamp nine times on the mat to activate prosperity.

Increasing Domestic Prosperity a Hundredfold

A multiarmed branch, painted gold, or a
sturdy potted tree or bush ∗ 100 small brass,
copper, or stainless-steel washers ∗ Red thread
or twine ∗ A gold candle ∗ A silver candle

TIMING

Sunrise

THE SPELL

∗ Make a pile of washers and pass both hands over them clockwise while saying continuously, *Ten, twenty, thirty, a hundredfold, increasing wealth I shall behold.*

∗ When you feel power throbbing through your fingers, attach the washers with the thread to the tree and say, *Prosperity tree, grow for me, a hundredfold, into my home bring silver and gold, that I/we may be blessed abundantly.*

∗ When all the washers are on the branch/plant, set it near the center/heart of your home where you/the family relax.

∗ Once a week, burn a gold and silver candle next to it and name the specific prosperity you need to enter your home.

A Red Ritual if Your Home and Those Within It Are Suffering from Financial Hardship

YOU WILL NEED

Red soft furnishings such as red cushions,
in the heart of the home ★ Three red candles placed in
a triangle on a table in the center of the relaxing area
★ Three red crystals placed in the center of the triangle

TIMING

Thursday

THE SPELL

* Light the candles, beginning at the apex of the triangle and continuing clockwise. Say the following words nine times, *More than sufficiency is there here, abundance and prosperity bring good cheer, all in the home is going well, of success and victory do I tell.*

* After five or ten minutes, blow out the candles and say the same words nine times, this time ending with nine rapid claps.

* Put the crystals in your purse/wallet, wear something red, and buy any high-quality red fruit. Then say, *I attract only the best, wealth not poverty envelops me, and only prosperity pours into me.*

A Viking Magick Prosperity and Abundance Bag for Your Home

YOU WILL NEED

A red candle on which you have etched invisibly with your index finger the wealth-generating rune, *Naudhiz* ✳ A red bag ✳ Dried bay leaves or sage ✳ Oats or grains in a sealed bag ✳ Three silver or gold coins ✳ A small twig ✳ Knotted sewing silk ✳ A twist of salt in foil

TIMING

New Year's Eve before midnight or any beginning of a month

THE SPELL

✳ Light the candle. Add each ingredient to the bag in turn while saying this old Viking abundance chant, *This bag I create and preserve for me, and also for my family, by Frigg, flax, flags and Frey, food, fuel, garments, wealth and health.*

✳ Secure the bag and blow out the candle.

✳ Hide the bag near the hearth/heart of your home, never touching it.

✳ Replace it after a year.

A Kitchen Ritual for Expanding Money

YOU WILL NEED

A flat white stone found outside your home
★ A shiny metal dish ★ A small orange-, cinnamon-,
lavender-, or lemon-scented candle set on the
stone ★ A supply of shiny coins

TIMING

Ongoing

THE SPELL

* Light the candle and place it on an accessible shelf in the kitchen, preferably near the stove/microwave. Then say, *Incubate, do not wait or hesitate, guardian stone, let abundance expand and constantly come.*

* Begin a coin circle around the candle with a single coin.

* Leave the candle to burn.

* Each week, replace the candle, repeat the spell, and add another coin to the circle.

* When the coin circle is complete, put one coin from it in your purse/wallet to spend. Replace the coin in the circle with a new coin as you continue to do the spell (the circle should always remain complete).

A Home Prosperity and Abundance Ritual

YOU WILL NEED

Any household items, such as household linen, china, special jewelry, or fancy clothes you keep or put away for special occasions or never use ⋆ Two white feathers

TIMING

Whenever domestic finances seem to be tight

THE SPELL

* Set your chosen high-quality item on a flat surface. Hold a feather in each hand and spiral them slowly and continuously while saying, *North, South, East, West, I attract only the best, I do not lock away my treasures, but attract abundance along with pleasures.*

* Continue to spiral the feathers slower and slower. Say the words slowly and quietly, until the words and movements slow into stillness and silence.

* Make an effort to use only the best-quality items you have in order to attract the best financial energies into your life.

A Furniture Polish Ritual to Bring in New Sources of Income to the Home and Family

YOU WILL NEED

Lavender or beeswax furniture polish ★ Two soft yellow cloths ★ A letter opener ★ Washing machine (or bathtub)

TIMING

A sunny day

THE SPELL

* Go from room to room, starting near the back of the house at the top and working downstairs toward the front door.

* Put a little polish on each suitable piece of furniture with the first cloth, then rub it in clockwise with the second cloth in circles, until the furniture shines. While doing this, say the following words in a continuous chant, *Enter here the sun, shine bright prosperity, gleaming and reflecting abundance, continuing shall it be.*

* With the polish, in the washing machine (or in a bathtub), draw a symbol of prosperity, a dollar sign, a flower, or the words *prosperity/wealth* using the letter opener.

* Put on the lid and wash the cloths.

A Sun and Moon Metal Spell for Bringing Ongoing Yearlong Prosperity

95

YOU WILL NEED

Four brass or gold small items for the sun and four silver for the moon ⋆ A soft yellow cloth ⋆ A small basket with a sparkly cloth inside

TIMING

When the sun and moon are both in the sky

THE SPELL

* Polish the brass or gold items one by one, saying, *Dawn, noon, sunset, midnight, day by day, prosperity shine and stay.*

* When they are gleaming, put them in the basket.

* Then polish the silver items one by one, saying, *Waxing, full, wane and dark time, moon by moon, may prosperity shine.*

* Add to the basket.

* Leave them under sun and moon for a few hours, then bring indoors, saying, *Sun and Moon, year by year shall prosperity come and remain here.*

* Each month light a gold and silver candle next to the basket.

Creating a Prosperity Garden Indoors or Out

YOU WILL NEED

A small waterfall feature (optional)

★ Any or all of basil, bay tree, bergamot, chamomile, ginger,
lavender, mint, orange tree, patchouli, rosemary, roses,
sage, sunflower seed, tarragon, thyme, and vetiver

★ Four moss agate, jade, or dendritic or tree agate crystals

★ Nine bamboo canes, mini if indoors ★ Scarlet cord

TIMING

Waxing moon, just before full moon

THE SPELL

* Indoors or outdoors, plant your herbs/seeds and bury the four crystals
around them in the soil.

* Place your bamboo canes in the soil above the crystals, each with nine
red cords tied around them.

* Place the water feature so the flow faces inward/toward the house
in the north.

* Facing your garden/indoor garden, with hands vertical and fingers
together, say softly, *Guardians of the home who protect with health and
wealth, as this garden grows, let abundance always rise not fall.*

To Keep Wealth Circulating Around Your Home and Life

YOU WILL NEED

A green, red, or blue semi-transparent fishing float
(often available in gift stores), an oversized large Christmas
shiny ornament, or a disco ball * Prosperity seeds
such as sunflower, cumin, poppy, or coriander

TIMING

Sunrise

THE SPELL

* Remove the hook from the top of the ball. Through the hole, insert the seeds while saying the following words slowly and continuously, *Fill all with your brightness, radiate your bountifulness, that abundance and wealth will grow and shimmer through my home all the year through.*

* When the ball is half full, hang it on a tree branch near the center of the garden or on an ornamental branch indoors where air and light will circulate round it.

* Each time you pass the ball, swirl it nine times clockwise, saying, *Nine by nine, make abundance mine.*

* Keep the ball polished.

Kindling the Fire if Domestic Finances Dip or Money is Pouring Out

YOU WILL NEED

Two safe candle containers, such as glass enclosing ones, preferably decorated with gold patterns, with sand in the bottom
* A supply of 24-hour burning sandalwood or patchouli or rose-scented candles

TIMING

Mid-to-late morning

THE SPELL

* Light the first candle in the first jar using a taper, saying, *So I kindle the long burning flame, so I rekindle in fortune's name, the flaring fire, to raise my fortunes ever higher.*

* When the candle is almost burned through, relight the taper from it and light the second candle in the second jar, repeating the spell words.

* Continue with fresh candles, alternating the jars for three, five, or seven days depending on how powerful the need is.

* Let the final candle burn down.

A Prosperity Heart of the Home Crystal Ritual to Hold on to Financial Stability in the Home and Family

YOU WILL NEED

A dish containing any seven of banded agate, clear quartz, green aventurine, citrine, jade, moss agate, dendritic or tree agate, rutilated quartz, tiger eye, or red tiger eye, set in the heart of the home   *   A pointed quartz crystal or clear quartz crystal massage wand   *   Seven candles

TIMING

Sunset

THE SPELL

* Light each candle so that light shines on the crystals.

* Touch in turn each crystal in the dish with the wand, saying, *May my home be a center of stability, no surprises, no demises, angst or anguish, crystals hold wealth fast within this dish. Seven candles, seven crystals, on you I call, on you I wish, to thrive, not just survive, shining forth as security.*

* Leave the candles to burn through.

* Repeat the spell weekly.

CHAPTER 7

Spells FOR Bringing Money Into THE Home Using Foods AND THE Kitchen

Domestic prosperity spells draw in money, resources, and opportunities for ourselves and family members and attract abundance, prosperity's twin sister. Spells involving food and drink foster abundance, which helps bring in actual money as well as a sense of well-being that can be shared. Indeed, by sharing our wealth with those who are deserving rather than with the financial or emotional vampires that we all encounter throughout our lives, we can create a cycle of abundance that replenishes itself.

By their very natures, many prosperity-attracting substances such as garlic and sage also carry built-in protection, happiness, and health-giving properties. Once activated as centers of abundance, the family table and kitchen magically draw in prosperity. The act of eating and drinking can thus serve as an opportunity to absorb wealth magick into our energy systems.

A Mother Earth Figs and Dates Abundance Ritual

A bowl of dried or fresh figs or dates with pits
* A beeswax candle * An old bowl
* Gold glitter

TIMING

The crescent moon

THE SPELL

* Place the figs/dates in front of the candle.

* Light the candle.

* Eat a fig or date, saying, *Fruit of wealth, fruit of richness, Mother Earth abundance, bring in everything.*

* Drop the fig/date pit in the bowl, sprinkle glitter on it, and, if you wish, eat one or two more, repeating the words and actions.

* Leave the candle to burn.

* Continue the spell each day with a fresh candle, until all the pits are in the bowl.

* Then add the rest of the glitter and drip candle wax into the bowl.

* Bury the bowl and contents in the earth saying, *I offer to Mother Earth her own for a prosperous and happy home.*

103

A Traditional Tomato Ritual for Bringing Prosperity and Abundance into the Home

YOU WILL NEED

A glass dish of ripening tomatoes placed in the
center of the kitchen table or work surface

TIMING

Ongoing

THE SPELL

* Hold your hands about half an inch over the bowl. With your palms
  flat and your fingers together, move your hands slowly over the bowl
  while saying, *Ripen to full maturity, draw in health and prosperity to me/
  my family.*

* Continue each day using the same words and actions.

* When the tomatoes ripen, hold one in each hand over the bowl of
  remaining tomatoes, saying, *Your ripeness brings prosperity, your richness
  shall my life impress, abundance draws in happiness.*

* Use the tomatoes in a salad or another dish while saying, *I take within
  your sweet prosperity, day by day and so abundance grows in every way.*

* Continue the spell whenever you wish.

Making an Abundance Basket to Bring All Manner of Good Things into Your Home and Life

A wicker or straw basket with a yellow cloth inside and sufficient golden foods and fruits to fill it, such as oranges, golden apples, small sealed packets of golden nuts, grains, or seeds ＊ A vase of fresh yellow flowers

TIMING

Ongoing

THE SPELL

* Add your golden foods and fruits to the basket in sunlight or yellow candlelight, saying, *Abundance give and abundance receive, so shall prosperity my life never leave.*

* Keep the basket where family, friends, and visitors can help themselves.

* Top up the basket regularly, replacing perishable items and scattering them outdoors for the birds or burying them.

* Whenever the flowers fade, scatter the petals outdoors, saying, *So shall abundance in my life regrow, set free to return as prosperity.*

A Family Meal Blessing to Bring Abundance to the Home

YOU WILL NEED

Yellow or gold candles placed around the room where you will eat ★ A gold candle placed in the center of the table ★ A yellow cloth for your table ★ Yellow, golden, or spicy foods, as part of the meal ★ A gold-colored bell

TIMING

Before you/family/friends come to sit at the table

THE SPELL

* Ring the bell six times around the table, saying, *I call with your golden sound, prosperity all around.*

* Light all the candles except the central one and say, *Candle light, shine bright, call prosperity to me/my family, bringing abundance, warmth and care, that laughter and happiness I/all can share.*

* Go into the kitchen and ring the bell over each food dish while repeating the first set of words.

* Light the central candle on the dining table and repeat the second set of words just before serving.

A Honey Spell to Ensure Sufficient Resources for You and Your Loved Ones

YOU WILL NEED

A dish of honey ✳ A spoon ✳ A beeswax candle on a flat holder or heatproof tray ✳ A dish of sunflower seeds ✳ A knife

TIMING

Sunset

THE SPELL

✳ Light the candle and hold the honey dish so that light shines into it. Say, *Honey Bee, let your sweetness enter me/my family, that I/we may in my life/ our lives increase see.*

✳ Eat a spoonful of honey, then repeat the words.

✳ As the wax melts on the tray, eat a few sunflower seeds and say the words again, dropping a few seeds in the wax.

✳ As it cools, use the knife to draw a bee around the seeds in the wax. When it cools, cut it out.

✳ Keep your wax bee on a high kitchen shelf until it crumbles.

✳ Eat the rest of the seeds and honey.

A Home or Workplace Ritual to Bring Short-Term and Long-Term Financial Opportunity

A mint tea bag ⁎ A cup or mug of hot water
⁎ Mint plants

TIMING

Wednesday and Thursday

THE SPELL

⁎ On Wednesday, pour the water on the tea bag. Stir five times, then stir three more times clockwise. With every stir, say, *Wealth and fortune enter here, opportunity does appear, in my home shall prosperity thrive, all good things do come alive.*

⁎ Sip the tea when brewed, saving a little in the bottom.

⁎ Stir the remains with the index finger of your right hand while naming how you most need prosperity.

⁎ Plant the fresh mint in pots in your kitchen or garden and sprinkle the remaining tea around the roots before adding the soil.

⁎ On Thursday, repeat the spell, but skip the planting. Sprinkle the remains of the contents around the plant while repeating the chant.

A Garlic Kitchen Ritual to Incubate Wealth

YOU WILL NEED

A string of garlic bulbs ✳ A knife
✳ A dish of salt ✳ A yellow candle

TIMING

Wednesday morning

THE SPELL

✳ Peel each garlic bulb so you have a smooth surface.

✳ Light the candle and sprinkle a little salt in the flame.

✳ Toss salt over the garlic string, shake it well, and say, *Garlic bring both health and wealth, salt sparkle, spread your bounty far and wide, that prosperity shall in my home reside.*

✳ On each garlic bulb, carve dollar signs or your local currency symbol, repeating the words for each bulb.

✳ Holding the garlic string by the ends, pass each bulb over, in front of, and behind the candle while repeating the words.

✳ Hang the garlic string in the kitchen, where air will circulate around it, until it shrivels. Replace it, but do not use this garlic for cooking.

A Manna Angel of Household Abundance Ritual for Increasing Family Resources in Hard Times

YOU WILL NEED

A bread mix or make your own bread
★ A kitchen knife ★ A dish of salt ★ A dish of
butter ★ A pot of honey and a spoon

TIMING

Before breakfast

THE SPELL

* Make a small loaf of bread. Before baking, write on top, MANNA, ANGEL OF ABUNDANCE, BRING MY HOME WEALTH.

* Cut a slice of bread and on it spread butter, saying, *Manna, angel of abundance, bring my home wealth, I ask not just for myself, but that with my loved ones I can share, Manna, I commit all to your care.*

* Add a spoonful of honey to the bread and repeat the words.

* Eat the bread and honey.

* Share the rest with your family or, if you're alone, crumble the bread for the birds and use the butter and honey in cooking.

* Repeat weekly until things improve.

A Crystal and Rice Wealth-Growing Ritual

YOU WILL NEED

A glass bowl of uncooked rice ✻ Three double-pointed
clear quartz crystals and a squarish tiger's eye
✻ A small hand mirror ✻ A gold candle
(to use if weather is overcast)

TIMING

A sunny day or use a gold candle

THE SPELL

✻ Place the three crystals on top of the uncooked rice in a triangle
  formation so the points almost touch, and place the tiger's eye
  in the center.

✻ Shine the mirror toward the sun or shine it into the gold candle.

✻ Then, as fast as possible, angle the mirror so the mirror is reflected into
  the bowl and say, *In the light of riches grow, in the brightness of wealth
  do shine, enough for my needs and more to show, that increasing fortunes
  shall be mine,*

✻ Leave the crystals in the bowl where light shines daily.

✻ When the rice is damp or discolored, replace it and wash the crystals.

A Salt and Rice Ritual to Exchange Bad Financial Luck in the Home for Good

YOU WILL NEED

Salt and uncooked rice mixed in a bowl

TIMING

Full moon day

THE SPELL

* Walk around the home, from back to front, while continuously shaking the bowl and saying, *Bad money fortunes come not here inside, you shall no longer in my home abide, no more worry no more fear, debt and darkness now are clear.*

* Open the front door and throw out the contents of the bowl as far as you can. If you're in an apartment, leave the premises first. While throwing, say, *Out you go, linger no longer, my good fortunes entering are much stronger.*

* Collect a new bowl of salt and rice.

* Keep it incubating in your kitchen. If things do not rapidly improve, repeat the spell after a week with this new bowl. Otherwise, throw it away after a week.

A Wealth Pomander for Speeding Up Financial Resources Coming into the Home

113

YOU WILL NEED

An orange ✳ Cloves ✳ A skewer
✳ Red ribbon ✳ Any dried mixed spices and
powdered seeds on a large plate

TIMING

Noon

THE SPELL

✳ Pierce the orange skin all over with the skewer to create small holes in the shape of dollar signs or the symbol of your local currency.

✳ Push cloves into the holes while saying, *In shall fly on golden wings, dollars* [or name currency] *from the wealth well springs.*

✳ Roll the completed pomander in the spice mix, repeating the words.

✳ Shake off any residual powder and wrap the ribbon around the pomander, securing it at the top with a large loop.

✳ Hang the pomander in a warm, dry place where air circulates, near the center of your home.

A Spice Rack Ritual for an Ongoing Flow of Financial Security and Stability

YOU WILL NEED

Two orange candles ✶ A spice rack containing
herbs or spice jars ✶ A twig from a fruit- or
nut-bearing tree ✶ Red ribbon

TIMING

Saturday before sunset

THE SPELL

* Light the candles one from the other and set them on either side of the spice rack.

* Touch each of the spice jars once, left to right, with the pointed end of the twig, saying for each, *To my finances, bring stability, to my money affairs, give security, the fertility of the tree, I transfer as wealth to me.*

* Do the same once more, right to left.

* Blow out the candles.

* Put the twig upright in a plant pot (outdoors or indoors) and tie it in the red ribbon.

* Use the herbs/spices in cooking. When they are all used, create more.

An Egg Prosperity Ritual to Call Extra Income to Your Home from Outside Sources

115

YOU WILL NEED

A hen's egg ✳ A knife ✳ Cloves, cumin, and pumpkin and sesame seeds mixed in a dish ✳ A green wax candle ✳ A green ribbon

TIMING

Early waxing moon

THE SPELL

✳ Cut off the top of the eggshell and drain the inside. Pour in water until it's clean, then leave it to dry.

✳ Light the candle and hold the dish of seeds in front of it, saying, *I bring into my home and life extra sources, new resources, calling in, let it begin.*

✳ Fill the eggshell with the seeds and repeat the words.

✳ Replace the lid of the egg, dripping green wax to seal it.

✳ Let the candle burn through.

✳ Tie the ribbon around the egg and secure it on top with a loop.

✳ Hang it above an outward-facing window for three months.

CHAPTER 8

Increasing Prosperity Through Speculation, Gambling, Games of Chance, Competitions, and the Lottery

Because of its uncertain nature, speculation can benefit enormously from spells. Speculation doesn't only mean gambling—it can also include consulting the most expensive brokers of stocks or shares or investing in get-rich-quick schemes with friends or family. When making tough decisions about moving or investing funds, spells can help guide us and tip the balance of fortune in our favor. Split-second intuition is the key to success for many speculators and gamblers. But this intuition, whether in business or gambling, can be strengthened if preceded by a spell and followed up with the recitation of a few powerful words.

Spells have always been associated with slanting the odds of chance. Since we know that thoughts can manifest in the process of sending out magical energies, then why not use spell energies to draw what we want to us? This claircognizant or psychic knowing, called "kenning" by the people of Scotland, can help us achieve our goals. Of course, big monetary gains can only be made if you possess one-hundred percent faith and focus. Speculation spells can be used to bring in the precise amount of money you require, but I've found that they often succeed in attracting more.

Spice Magick for Major Speculation or Investments

YOU WILL NEED

Six different powdered spices in small jars
* Cornstarch or unscented baby powder * A red candle
* A bowl and spoon * Orange or frankincense
essential oil * A small glass jar with a lid

TIMING

Wednesday after dawn

THE SPELL

* Light the candle and say, *Spices hot, candle fire, make profitability rise ever higher.*

* In the bowl, mix two tablespoons of each spice plus two tablespoons of cornstarch and a few drops of orange oil. Repeat the words as you perform the mixing.

* Hold the mix in the bowl so candlelight falls on it. Say, *Accumulate and speculate, I gain, no pain.*

* Put the mixture in the jar and close it. Keep it with your financial papers or near your computer.

* Let the candle burn.

* On the morning of the speculation, sprinkle a little mix outside, close to where you'll be speculating.

For the Successful Speculation of a Family Consortium or Where Investment by Others Is Essential

YOU WILL NEED

A separate small container of sand for each potential investor (including yourself), different colors if possible ★ A small scoop ★ A larger clear container with a lid

TIMING

Wednesday morning

THE SPELL

* With the scoop, add the sand from each jar in turn to the larger jar. As you're doing this, name yourself, then name the other investors each jar represents. Say, *Accumulate, make more, let profit inwards pour, together and not separate, we shall not wait, and so I call on Lady Luck to smile on our endeavor.*

* When all the sands are in the jar, put on the lid.

* Swirl it clockwise, once for each investor, and repeat the words three times.

* Go outdoors, and, holding the jar to the skies, say, *Investment, speculation, rise higher and higher, for to success together we do aspire.*

For Speculation or Assessment Where There Are Unknown Factors You Must Build In

Six dice * A copy of a paper connected with the transaction * A small yellow purse or drawstring bag * A yellow candle

TIMING

The brightest time of the day

THE SPELL

* Light the candle, and say, *Flame the way to success bright, unknown factors bring to light, and so I extinguish any danger, from down-turning forces or dishonest stranger.*

* Extinguish the candle and relight it. Toss the dice in your closed hands 36 times, counting aloud, and say, *Six by six, does the trick, roll the dice, they do not fall, take a chance and winner takes all.*

* Fold the paper around the dice into a parcel, securing it with tape if necessary, and keep it in the bag. Toss the bag six times and repeat the second set of words six times.

A Spell to Double Your Money Within a Specified Period for an Investment or Speculation

YOU WILL NEED

Three one-dollar coins or similar value coins in your own currency

TIMING

The last day of the month and the first day of the new month

THE SPELL

* Toss the first coin from your open-cupped hands, saying, *Double your money if not overnight, double your money when it is right* [name specified period desired for return].

* Take the coin outside, throwing it as far as you can, say, *Cast my fortunes to the winds, double my money, double the wins.*

* The first day of the month, toss the two remaining coins in your hands, repeating the words.

* Outdoors, cast the coins away, once again saying the words.

* If you wish (or if you're seeking a fast return), continue with four dollars the third day and eight the fourth day. Make sure to repeat the words as you're throwing the coins.

A Lucky Charm for Any Form of Speculation, Gambling, Competition, or Game of Chance

YOU WILL NEED

A Lucky Hand root (the root of a rare orchid, considered the luckiest gambling symbol. Toxic, so keep it away from children)
* Patchouli essential oil * A small leather pouch
* Red cord * A plate * A 24-hour burning candle

TIMING

Sunset

THE SPELL

* Light the candle, saying, *Lucky Hand root, you promise me, immense good fortune and prosperity, with oil I make this offering, asking for luck in everything* [name specific results needed].

* Place your Lucky Hand root on the plate, sprinkle it with oil, and repeat the words.

* Leave it in candlelight until the candle burns through.

* Secure it in the pouch with three knots, saying, *So do I enclose my good fortune, to be released at my command, bring to me the greatest luck, this I ask, Lucky Root Hand.*

* Open the bag whenever you need good luck.

Making a Lucky Game of Chance Magick Bag

YOU WILL NEED

A green candle ✶ A Lucky Hand root (optional)
✶ A miniature ten of diamonds playing card ✶ Dried sage in
a tiny bag ✶ A silver dollar or coin ✶ A gambling chip
✶ A green aventurine or amazonite crystal ✶ A white
drawstring bag ✶ A white cord ✶ A little
whiskey, port, or malt wine

TIMING

After sunset Wednesday, working by candlelight

THE SPELL

✳ Place all the items in the bag or purse in silence. Add a drop or two
of alcohol.

✳ Close the bag or purse with the cord, tying it with three knots. Say,
*Fortune favor all my ventures, luck make chance a certainty, that what
I speculate or risk, in my favor always shall be.*

✳ Take the bag with you when gambling or speculating or place it on top
of competition entries, etc.

✳ Replace it every year and a day, using the same contents.

Using Lucky Crystals to Win
Money or Good Prizes

YOU WILL NEED

Three green aventurine or amazonite crystals in a triangle
* Three vetiver or patchouli incense cones, placed in a
triangle surrounding the crystals * A green scarf

TIMING

Each full moon

THE SPELL

* Light the incense cones and say, *Within the power of the triple moon, let these crystals fill with good fortune.*

* When the incense cones are burned and the ash is cool, place the crystals in the scarf, add the ash, and fold the scarf into an enclosing triangle secured with three knots.

* Leave the cloth on an indoor window ledge until morning.

* Keep the knotted cloth with any competition entries or raffle tickets.

* Each full moonlight unknot the scarf and repeat the spell, adding more ash until the scarf is full.

* Then wash the crystals and the cloth and begin again.

A Spell to Win Bingo, Lottery, and Raffles

Three pieces of real gold, such as earrings ★ A glass dish
filled with cloves or dried juniper berries ★ Three gold
candles placed in a triangle around the gold
and dish ★ A small bag or purse

TIMING

Two nights before and the night of the full moon

THE SPELL

126

* On night one, light the first candle and say, *Growing moon, gold increased be, that immense good winnings I shall see.*

* When the candle is burned down, add the first piece of gold to the bowl.

* On night two, light the next candle, repeat the spell, and add the second piece of gold.

* On the night of the full moon, light the third candle, repeat the spell, and add the remaining gold.

* Raise the bowl to the moon three times, saying, *Lady Moon, fill with power, my golden fortune at this hour.*

* Keep the bowl in a warm place.

For Winning Any Game of Chance

The Wheel of Fortune card from a small-sized tarot pack
or a joker from a miniature playing card pack
∗ The numbers for your chosen game on separate
slips of paper, spread clockwise around the
outside of the card ∗ A small wallet

TIMING

The morning before taking part in a game of chance

THE SPELL

∗ Touch the Wheel of Fortune/joker and say, *Wheel of Fortune upward turn, bring the win that I do yearn.*

∗ Touch each number clockwise and end by saying, *Lucky numbers be drawn to me, as in this spell I do count three, two, one, the right numbers come.*

∗ Put the card in the wallet, saying, *Whenever I touch you wheel within, I will activate a win.*

∗ Immediately before a game or bet, touch the wallet and allow the winning numbers to come to you.

To Make You a Winner at Cards

A new pack of cards to keep for spells and games,
unless you already have a lucky pack
* A gold-colored medallion or medal

TIMING

When first you acquire the pack if new, or Wednesday if old

THE SPELL

* Shuffle the pack and gently, without marking the cards, rub the back of each one with the medal/medallion while saying the following words softly and continuously, *Winner takes all, a flawless hand, luck and skill together band, the right cards dealt, perfectly played, my fortune made.*

* Return the cards to their sleeve or the bag in which you keep them.

* Before the game, put one hand on the top of the unopened pack and one on the bottom. While cradling the pack, say the following words softly, *My call, the cards my way fall, winner takes all.*

* Re-empower the cards monthly (or more often, if you play frequently).

To Win on Gaming Machines

YOU WILL NEED

A handful of gaming chips or tokens bought before the game

TIMING

Before the game and while facing a machine

THE SPELL

* Hold the chips in your closed hands. Shake them nine times and, in your mind, say the following words nine times, *I have won, it shall be done, all shall align, fortune is mine.*

* As you use each of the empowered chips, repeat the words in your mind.

* When you have used them all, if you wish, empower more, this time including any you have gained as winnings.

A Cassiel Archangel of Good Fortune
Ritual to Win Prizes in the Lottery

YOU WILL NEED

A pointed purple amethyst or yellow citrine placed
in the center of a circle ★ Squares of paper, each
containing one of the possible lottery numbers, written,
placed face down, and mixed and put in a circle

TIMING

Whenever you feel lucky

THE SPELL

* Pass your hands in clockwise circles an inch above the center of the number circle, saying, *Lucky I feel, lucky shall I be, the luckiest numbers Cassiel, choose for me.*

* Take the crystal and hold it an inch over each of the numbers clockwise in turn (make sure the pointed-end of the crystal is facing down). Do this until you feel pulling or vibrations over the right number of squares.

* These are your numbers for one lottery attempt.

* Thank Cassiel for blessings to be received.

* As soon as possible, buy your lottery ticket using your lucky numbers.

To Do Well in Currency Exchange Transactions if Rates Are Fluctuating Rapidly

YOU WILL NEED

A currency note in each of the two currencies you are exchanging. Repeat the spell if further currencies are involved

TIMING

Before exchanging money or speculating on currency deals

THE SPELL

* Hold a currency note in each hand and exchange them rapidly from hand to hand while repeatedly chanting the following words faster and faster, *Swapping and changing, advantageously exchanging, get the best rate, never too late,*
most profit making, go for the upswing.

* When you can chant and move no faster, close your hands fast around both currency notes and say, *Now is the time, to make the deal mine.*

* As soon as possible, make the transaction.

* Keep the currency notes together. Tie them to one another with an elastic band so you remember not to spend them.

A Spell to Win a Competition or Contest Where the Prize Would Transform Your Life

Ten brightly colored beads with holes in them
for threading * A string for the beads

TIMING

A few hours before the competition, contest, or prize draw

THE SPELL

* Tie one end of the string in three knots, saying, *Three by three, luck's with me.*

* Thread the beads one by one on the string, saying, *Ten to one, my prize is won, one, two, three, my desired result I do see, four, five, six, success I mix, seven, eight, nine, the desired result soon will be mine, ten to one, the prize to me comes.*

* Tie the other end with three knots and carry or wear the beads when you buy the ticket or enter the contest. While doing this, repeat the following phrase ten times in your mind, *Ten to one, my prize is won.*

For Success at Horse Racing

YOU WILL NEED

The name of your chosen horse written in green on white paper and also on a white envelope ⋆ Pins and a small magnet ⋆ Dragon's Blood and frankincense incense sticks ⋆ A green wax candle

TIMING

Just before placing a bet

THE SPELL

* Light the candle and the incense behind the paper.

* Drop some pins on the paper and collect them with the magnet, saying, *Winnings come to me, swift shall* [name horse] *be and easily romp to victory.*

* Wrap the pins still on the magnet in the paper and roll the paper toward you. Put the paper (with the pins) in the envelope and secure it with hot green wax.

* Write on the envelope, THE WINNER.

* Blow out the candle and leave the incense to burn.

* Keep it with the betting slip until the race is done.

To Tell You When to Take Your Winnings and Go

YOU WILL NEED

A natural beeswax or grainy purple candle
★ Kitchen paper or a plate ★ Dried sage
★ A letter opener

TIMING

Before you go out gambling

THE SPELL

* Sprinkle a layer of herbs on the paper or plate. Write in the herbs, TEMPTATION BEWARE. LET ME SHOW CARE.

* Roll the candle backwards and forwards in the herbs, saying continuously, *Let me be wise, come home with my winnings, otherwise I will lose them and be back at the beginning.*

* When some herbs have stuck to the candle, light the candle and repeat both sets of words.

* Let the candle burn through.

* When cool dispose of the spilled wax, saying, *Temptation is no more. I close that door.*

* If you are tempted to keep playing, repeat all the spell words in your mind as you walk away with your winnings.

To Change Your Luck at Speculation and Gambling if You Always Lose and Feel Jinxed

YOU WILL NEED

A green candle

TIMING

Early Sunday

THE SPELL

* Cross and uncross your fingers behind your back nine times, saying, *Jinx, jinx, jinx, Three by three, unjinxed now shall I be. Good luck in gambling/speculation shall I see.*

* With your little (money) finger, invisibly trace the trident of the planet/god Neptune all over the unlit candle. Neptune has the power to turn your financial luck and bring you good fortune in speculation and gambling.

* Light the candle and keep crossing and uncrossing your fingers while repeating the words faster and faster until the words jumble.

* When you can go no faster, clap your hands over the candle three times and blow it out.

* When the candle is cool, invisibly redraw the Neptune glyph on the wax and leave the candle to burn.

CHAPTER 9

Property Investment: Buying AND Selling Homes, Businesses, AND Land; Building Homes AND Making Renovations

While buying property has traditionally proven to be an excellent step toward longer-term prosperity, it is also an area linked strongly to emotion, unless you happen to be buying properties to renovate and sell or rent out. Buying a home, especially a first home, whether a modest apartment or a dream house, represents a significant emotional and financial investment and may have been preceded by years of careful saving.

Property offers a nest egg for the future. Even in the face of market fluctuations, property ownership can offer you a more secure financial position. Spells for downturns in the economy can stir energies to make your property or business more visible and desirable to a wider range of buyers. In addition, these spells can help you attract the right agents and realtors to handle the sale or rental of your property.

For all these spells, if you can't acquire the ingredients suggested, you can substitute with all-purpose white candles, clear quartz or amethyst crystals, or rose or lavender incense. Instead of herbs or petals, split teabags can be used. The baking or seasonings section of your local supermarket should carry many spices and herbs in dried form.

To Stir the Energies for a Home or Business Sale if the Need to Sell is Urgent and Offers Are Nonexistent or Too Low

YOU WILL NEED

A metal canister of uncooked rice
* A small amount of molasses or honey in a tiny sealed bag and placed within the canister

TIMING

Full moon or a Sunday afternoon

THE SPELL

* Hold the closed canister between your hands. Shake it nine times while saying the following words faster and faster, *Half a pound of two dollar* [or traditionally two penny] *rice, half a pound of treacle, speed good offers and make them stick, send eager buyers and send them real quick.*

* Using your writing hand, bang nine times on the canister's top while saying the following words nine times (end the words with a band), *Send them real quick and make offers stick.*

* Use the contents of the canister in cooking.

A Second Ritual to Speed Up Your Sale in a Slow Market

YOU WILL NEED

A glass jar with a lid ＊ Sesame seeds in a container ＊ A red candle ＊ A map of the area from which you seek buyers (it could be a world map)

TIMING

Wednesday

THE SPELL

* Light the candle. Add a handful of seeds to the empty jar.

* Shake the jar quickly ten times while saying, *Speed up the market, speed up the sale, let a swift transaction soon prevail.*

* Blow out the candle.

* Relight the candle and repeat the spell continuously until the jar is half full.

* Leave the candle burning and tip the seeds from the jar over the map, saying, *Come from near, from far away, come on a visit and decide to stay, buy my home profitably, make an offer speedily.*

* Carefully carry the map outdoors and scatter the seeds in your garden.

To Sell a Home or Business Premises
Swiftly and Profitably

Six blue howlite crystals and one white howlite crystal

Wednesday

* In your open-cupped hands, carry the crystals to the center of the home/ business premises. Visit every room, first upstairs, then downstairs, then the front door. While carrying this out, say, *Purchasers come swiftly, buyers come profitably, in these crystals I call you to see, what a wonderful home/business this for you will be.*

* Return to the center of the home/business premises.

* Hold out the crystals in your non-writing hand. With the index finger of your writing hand, invisibly draw an eye over the crystals. Repeat the words as you carry this out.

* Leave the crystals in a pot outside the front door for 24 hours. Then bring them indoors and place the blue ones on window ledges and the white one above the front door.

To Sell a Home or Business You Are Reluctant to Leave but Know You Must

YOU WILL NEED

A wide-necked waterproof sealable jar
★ Three small items associated with happy
memories ★ A purple cord ★ Scissors

TIMING

Waning moon

THE SPELL

* Hold each item in turn and say, *You hold for me fond memories, you tie me to this place, but you know I must let go, and so I you release.*

* Seal the jar and knot the cord around it while repeating the words.

* Now cut the knots, saying, *I cut the bonds so fond, that hold me to the past, I keep the pleasure of each treasure, but let you go at last.*

* Bury the sealed jar in a pot or earth outside the front door.

* When you sell, dig up the jar, wash the outside, and take the items to your new home.

To Sell a Home When You Are Locked in a Chain of Buyers or Sellers

YOU WILL NEED

An old jewelry chain or necklace with links
* Pliers or pruning shears * A picture of the house you are
selling and next to it pictures or names of other properties
holding up the chain * A small blue bag or purse

TIMING

Early waxing moon

THE SPELL

* Cut the chain over the pictures so the individual links fall one
  by one on the pictures. Say, *Break the holdups, sever the chain,
  that straightforward proceedings shall remain.*

* Shake the paper gently, repeating the words ten times. Then,
  one by one, add the links to the bag or purse.

* Keep the bag with any sale papers or near your computer. Before
  entering into further negotiations, shake the closed bag ten times,
  saying the words ten times.

When You Are Made an Unreasonably Low Offer but Are Pressured to Take It

YOU WILL NEED

Six one-cent coins and six one-dollar coins, or similar coins in your local currency ✶ A purple candle and a white one

TIMING

When you receive an unreasonable offer

THE SPELL

* Light the purple candle and put the cent coins in a circle around it, saying, *Too cheap, though I am pressurized to leap, yet will I keep the faith, hold out for what I know my property/business is worth. I need not accept loss or dearth.*

* Add one dollar coin between each cent coin around the circle. Repeat the words during each placement.

* Then light the white candle from the purple one and put that in the center of the coins, repeating the words.

* Extinguish the purple candle and leave the white one to burn.

* Repeat the spell weekly until you get the right offer.

To Easily and Favorably Obtain a Loan for a Home or Business

A printed-out copy of the loan application
★ A pair of scissors ★ A small handheld electric fan ★ An envelope ★ A blue pen

TIMING

Thursday morning

THE SPELL

* Light the candle and hold the loan application in both hands in front of the candle, saying, *May approval be given to us/me, favorably, swiftly and easily, that I/we may make real our/my dream sooner than can possibly seem.*

* Cut the printout of the loan application into small pieces. With the fan, blow the shredded paper towards you while saying, *Come to me soon, swiftly and easily.*

* Put the shredded paper into the envelope and seal it, writing on the front, *Loan approved in full, swiftly and easily.*

* Leave it in front of the candle until the candle is burned and keep the envelope with the original loan application.

To Boost Your Savings if You Never Seem to Have Enough No Matter How Hard You Try

YOU WILL NEED

A lidded box ★ An open padlock and chain
★ Gold or silver coins ★ A green candle

TIMING

Thursday

THE SPELL

* Light the candle, open the box, and say, *Inward much does flow, outward little goes, accumulate, till savings become great, I cannot wait.*

* Put in a handful of coins and blow out the candle.

* Leave the padlock and chain in front of the box and touch it, saying, *No locks or keys will stand between my dreams and me.*

* Repeat the spell each day until all the coins are in the box.

* On the last day, leave the candle to burn.

* Place the open padlock inside the box and add the money to your savings.

A Spell to Speed Up Renovations if You Want to Sell or Rent Out a Property, Whether or Not You Are Doing the Renovations Yourself

YOU WILL NEED

Six orange carnelians * A bowl in which you
have soaked fragrant orange flowers

TIMING

Tuesday

THE SPELL

* Sprinkle flower water over the crystals, saying, *Let all be fixed and fast, this work just cannot last, remove all obstacles in the way, may it be completed soon if not right away.*

* While repeating the words, sprinkle flower water all around the areas being renovated.

* If possible, place the carnelians separately behind areas to be plastered, under floorboards being replaced, or taped under the doormat. Say the words again as you complete these actions.

* Leave the flowers in any remaining water in the center of the home, and when they fade, cast the petals outside with any water still in the bowl.

If Prospective Buyers Pull Out or Initial Interest is Not Followed Up

YOU WILL NEED

Four incense sticks in a square ★ A picture of your
home, in the center of the incense square ★ A container
filled with sand ★ Sesame or any fine seeds ★ Glue

TIMING

Waxing moon

THE SPELL

* Light the incense sticks and say the following words for each, *May buyers be blown in and not depart, may a sale be completed and not just start.*

* Pass each incense stick around the picture clockwise, then remove it from the square and say, *I take away all obstacles to a fast and profitable sale, I call in buyers to remain and not to fail.*

* Cover the picture with glue, sprinkle seeds on it, and say, *Buyers, come from all around, with offers that will me astound.*

* Extinguish each incense stick lighted-end down in the pot.

* Keep the picture where light will shine on it.

For Building Your Dream Property as a Home and Future Nest Egg

YOU WILL NEED

A red bag ✻ Six gold- or silver-colored coins ✻ Dried rose petals ✻ Dried lavender or chamomile ✻ A mini sagebrush or cedar smudge

TIMING

Crescent moon

THE SPELL

✻ Put each item into the bag. Close and knot it, saying, *Enough for my needs and a little more, health, happiness, by the score, a home to love, a nest egg too, to sustain me/us my/our whole life/lives through.*

✻ Light the smudge and spiral the smoke around the whole area of the future house (or through its half-finished rooms) while repeating the words. Begin and end where the front door will be.

✻ Hide the bag, bricked in if possible, behind the hearth or a wall of the main living area.

✻ Before the main living area wall is painted, write your/your family name in a color that can be painted over.

Spell for Finding the Right Real Estate Agent or Waking Yours Up If S/He is Being Lazy or Incompetent

YOU WILL NEED

The business card of the lazy agent
* A fireproof pot * A box of pearls
* A detailed map of your home area

TIMING

Tuesday

THE SPELL

* Shake the business card in closed hands ten times, saying, *Lazy Bones, this just won't do, shape up or I'll get rid of you.*

* Scatter the pearls on the map, saying, *Come from far, come from near, a good agent whose intent is clear, to sell my home, and sell it fast, and profitably is all I ask.*

* Tear up the business card, burn it in the pot, saying, *Lazy Bones, get inspired, act smart or you'll be fired.*

* Scoop up the pearls and give your agent a final warning. Check where most of the pearls fell on the map. Consider hiring an agent from this area.

For Finding the Right Piece of Land in Your Chosen Area That Will Bring Long-Term Profit

YOU WILL NEED

A pot of soil from the chosen area * Three jade crystals
* A green plant * A crystal pendant or pendulum

TIMING

Three days before the full moon

THE SPELL

* Put your hands around the plant and say, *My ideal land shall through the years in value grow, and in long term great profit show.*

* Place the plant in the soil and bury the crystals at the base of the plant while repeating the words.

* Hold the pendulum/pendant just above the plant and say the words again.

* Repeat the spell for the next two days.

* On the night of the full moon, do the spell, then hold your pendulum over a map of the chosen area, noting where it swings most powerfully.

* As soon as possible, start your search there. When you buy, bury the plant and the crystals in the land.

For Getting Your Offer Accepted on a Home or Business if You Suspect the Vendor is Playing Tricks

YOU WILL NEED

The Justice card from a tarot deck or ten of diamonds from playing cards ★ Your offer written in blue on white paper beneath the card ★ Four blue candles placed in a square around the card

TIMING

Thursday

THE SPELL

* Hold the card between your hands, turning it over ten times saying, *Fair Play, an honest deal, I don't mind paying, if the negotiation's real.*

* Lighting each candle in turn clockwise, blow softly into each flame, saying, *Deal true, put your cards on the table, I'm offering you as much as I am able.*

* Clap ten times while saying the second set of words faster and faster.

* Blow out all the candles at once and clap a final time.

* Keep the card with you in your wallet when negotiating.

For Finding a Bargain in the Place You Want to Live if Funds Are Tight

YOU WILL NEED

A double-sided hand/makeup mirror on a stand,
one side that magnifies ★ A white cloth
★ A bowl of clear water

TIMING

Saturday, when the light is brightest

THE SPELL

* Dip the index finger of your writing hand into the water and use it to write faintly on the magnified mirror surface. Write the name of the chosen place (the name should fill the screen). Then say, *Let me find the ideal home, where I would love to be, though my funds are limited, let me the right place see.*

* Now flip the mirror over. On the other side, use the water to write, in small letters, the maximum price you can afford to pay.

* Use your cloth to polish the mirror in clockwise circles, first the magnified side, then the other side. As you're doing this, repeat the words softly and continuously, until both sides of the mirror are dry.

* Hang the cloth outdoors to dry and look in both sides of the mirror, repeating the above chant before bargain hunting.

CHAPTER 10

Turning an Interest or Hobby into a Lucrative Second Career or Business

W e all have special talents that can be, in time, transformed into monetary opportunities. Perhaps these gifts were pushed to the background by the demands of a regular job or family. Later in life, they may finally have the chance to reemerge.

Home-based business ventures are on the rise. With the help of the internet and social media, your talents can become a viable alternative to conventional employment. With the help of a spell, you can attract customers and find guidance and assistance in choosing the right business to start, obtaining a loan, and managing the business's growth.

A spell can also give you the confidence to try your luck in what may seem like an overcrowded market, whether it's publishing books, restoring antiques, or making beautiful quilts or metal sculptures. It may be that your own unique approach leads you to stand out from the pack. The only limits are those of your own ingenuity.

To Turn a Talent or Interest into a Lucrative Business

YOU WILL NEED

A sample of your work, or if large, a photo of your work * A printout of a successful website or picture of a similar product or outlet * One each of red, yellow, green, and blue ribbons * Red, yellow, green, and blue candles placed behind the ribbons, with the pictures placed side by side between them

TIMING

Crescent moon

THE SPELL

* Set the sample on top of the website picture.

* Light the candles, first red, saying, *Like to like, give power to my enterprise.*

* Light yellow, saying, *Like to like, that my success will rise.* Light green, saying, *Like to like, to the skies.* Finally, light the blue one and say, *That my product/business will prosper likewise.*

* Knot the ribbons around the sample and printout, repeating the words.

* Leave the candles to burn.

* Keep the sample and printout knotted together in your workroom.

To Make Your Advertising and Publicity Attract Buyers, Both on and Beyond the Internet

YOU WILL NEED

A sample or photo of what you are selling
★ A large mirror ★ Six small, gold candles,
along the edge of the mirror

TIMING

Just before sunrise

THE SPELL

* Light the candles left to right. While standing behind them, look into the mirror and say, *So am I filled with light, my product will all delight.*

* Hold up your product/photo to reflect in the mirror, saying, *Visible be across land and sea, and close at hand, let my product/services be in huge demand.*

* As morning light enters the mirror, say, *The light grows, all will know my creations, come to me buyers, no hesitation.*

* Blow out the candles fast.

* Leave your product/picture propped in front of the mirror for 24 hours.

To Have the Confidence to Launch Yourself in the Marketplace

YOU WILL NEED

A business card or the name of your potential company written in gold on white ✳ Two white feathers ✳ A hole punch and white string ✳ A balloon or kite

TIMING

Waxing moon

THE SPELL

* Holding a feather in each hand, waft them in spirals over the card flat on the table, saying softly and continuously, *I believe in myself, I believe in my gifts, as I sell/do more, my confidence lifts.*

* When you feel the power building inside you, attach the card and feathers with the string to a kite or balloon and go outdoors.

* Release the balloon/kite, saying, *My confidence does soar and rise, I reach out in faith and aim for the skies.*

If Customers or Clients are Slow in Coming at First or You Experience a Downturn

YOU WILL NEED

Two pieces of white paper and a gold
pen * A small plastic container

TIMING

Saturday

THE SPELL

* Write on the first piece of paper, Unblock the locks, let orders flow, let my venture [Name] grow and grow.

* Fold the paper until it's small. Fill the container halfway with water and add in the paper. Place the container in the freezer for 24 hours.

* Remove the container from the freezer and let it thaw. Throw the soggy paper away and tip out the water.

* Now, on the second paper, write, Let light illumine, bring orders in, that I will shine, and business win.

* Leave the second paper where natural light will shine on it. Every Saturday thereafter, burn a gold candle next to the paper until the candle burns through. Continue doing this until things improve.

A Mehiel, Angel of Writers and Poets, Ritual to Get Your First Book or Poetry Collection Published

YOU WILL NEED

Seven white candles in a circle * A sample of
your work in the center of the candles
* A small, clear quartz crystal angel or crystal

TIMING

Seven consecutive days (any time of the year)

THE SPELL

* Light the first candle, saying, *Mehiel, who guides the pen, to my book/ poems open the door, that I may the right publisher find, who will love my work and ask for more.*

* Pass the angel/crystal around the candle, repeating the words. Blow out the candle.

* Leave the angel/crystal on top of the book/printout.

* Next day, set the angel/crystal outside the candle. Light an extra candle each day, repeating the spell.

* On day seven, when all seven candles are alight, leave them to burn through.

* Keep your angel/crystal with your work or near your writing computer.

* Hold it, saying the words before sending your work to a publisher.

To Sell Beautiful Artifacts, Artwork, or Your Crafts on the Internet or by Mail Order

YOU WILL NEED

A photo of what you sell ⋆ Two rose
incense sticks ⋆ A bowl of water

TIMING

Friday

THE SPELL

* Light your incense sticks and, while holding one in each hand, pass them in the air over either side of the photo in clockwise spirals while saying the following words continuously nine times, *A thing of beauty is a joy forever, may my artifacts/crafts sell across land and sea, let their loveliness bring happiness to others, and as profit return to me.*

* Now plunge the incense in the hand with which you write into the water so it hisses.

* Turn over the photo. Using the wet incense stick tip in your writing hand, write on the back of the photo, Success through beauty be mine.

* When it is dry, pin the picture by your computer/workstation.

To Earn Money Teaching Your Gifts to Others

YOU WILL NEED

A bubble blower and bubbles

TIMING

Wednesday morning

THE SPELL

* Go outdoors and stir the bubbles with the blower five times clockwise and five times counterclockwise, then five more times clockwise. While doing this, say, *My expertise shall I guide and teach, so my talents far and wide will reach.*

* Blow a bubble and name your main area of expertise and target audience.

* Continue to blow bubbles, adding any extra talents and potential teaching markets, workshops, etc.

* When all the bubbles are gone, hold the bubble blower to your lips and whisper through it, *So my expertise shall I guide and teach, so my talents far will reach, my teaching others will inspire. Rise to the skies, rise ever higher.*

* Blow for the final time any residue on the bubble blower.

To Open a Party or Cooking Business

YOU WILL NEED

Some cakes or party products you have made,
on a plate ★ A circle of five small yellow and five small red candles,
placed alternately around the cakes ★ Paper flowers or garlands

TIMING

Wednesday

THE SPELL

* Decorate the room with the paper flowers or garlands.

* Starting with the candle farthest away, light the candles one from
  the other, clockwise, saying, *I spread and shed happiness, my party/catering
  business offers no less, joyously, brings profitability, and will a promising
  career provide for me.*

* Repeat the words nine times, faster and faster, circling your hands in the
  air as you face the cakes. On the final time, blow out all the candles and
  make a wish for your business.

* Eat one cake and, throughout the day, share the rest with others.

To Start or Take Over a Store Where You Can Sell Your Products and Those of Others

A sheet of yellow or orange paper
★ A black pen ★ Scissors ★ Eleven small,
clear crystals and one larger red one

TIMING

Sunday, preferably in sunlight

165

THE SPELL

* Draw the sun glyph on the paper so it almost fills it.

* Run your finger around the rim of the sun circle, clockwise once, while saying, *Sun shine, make success mine, sun glow, let my new premises with customers grow.*

* Cut around the outside of the black rim, repeating the words until the sun sign is free.

* Attach the sun glyph to a wall facing the entrance. Under the front doormat, place the twelve crystals in a circle (with red in the middle), forming the sun symbol. These can also be placed on an outward-facing window or window ledge.

To Get the Right Grants and Loans to Turn Your Interest into a Business

YOU WILL NEED

A printout version of a possible loan or grant application on thin white paper ✴ Six gold or silver coins or Chinese divination coins in a row, left to right, under the center of the paper ✴ A wide-tipped pencil

TIMING

Sunday

THE SPELL

✴ With the pencil on top of the paper, rub over the coins under the paper, left to right, to leave their imprints on top of the paper, saying, *Let me an impression make, let the authority* [name bank, etc.] *me seriously take, that funds be released to me, swiftly and easily.*

✴ Now, rub the index finger of the hand with which you write over each imprint left to right, repeating the words.

✴ Keep the imprinted paper next to your computer or under the application.

To Launch an Invention or Innovative Product

YOU WILL NEED

Two large mirrors propped on surfaces, so you can stand between them ⋆ A wide-beamed flashlight ⋆ Your invention if small or a photo of it if larger

TIMING

As darkness falls

THE SPELL

* Stand between the mirrors and face the one on your left. Hold your invention/photo in your writing hand and hold the flashlight in the other.

* Switch on the flashlight. Wave it in clockwise spirals over your invention, then shine it into the mirror on your left in spirals. While doing this, say the following words softly and continuously, *Let my invention with brilliance shine, that recognition will be mine.*

* While facing the other mirror, again spiral the flashlight over your invention/photo. Then wave it over the second mirror in spirals, once more saying the words softly and continuously.

* Switch off the flashlight.

* Leave the invention/photo between the mirrors until morning light fills the mirrors.

To Turn a Love of Outdoor Activities and Sports into an Adventure Center

YOU WILL NEED

Ten small bouncy balls in a row
★ A wall ★ An empty space

TIMING

Waxing moon

THE SPELL

* Bounce the first ball against the wall quickly ten times while (also quickly) saying the following words ten times, *Open for me.*

* Throw the ball over your right shoulder.

* Repeat the actions just as quickly for each ball, but change the words. For ball two, *say, my destiny,* for ball three, say, *that adventure I will see.* For four, say, *profitably,* for five, say, *that my adventure center,* for six, say, *will prove a profitable venture,* for seven, say, *laughter, skill,* for eight, say, *brings a fill,* for nine, say, *of high profile and success,* for ten, say, *money and happiness.*

* Leave the balls for a child to find.

To Fulfill the Dream to Establish a Healing Sanctuary or Retreat

YOU WILL NEED

A picture of the place where you would like to open your sanctuary * Four lily-, orchid-, or rose-scented candles, one in each corner * A vase of lilies, orchids, or white roses * A heatproof pot

TIMING

Sunday

THE SPELL

* Scatter the petals from the flowers on the picture, saying, *I call to this my sanctuary, my place of healing and peace, flowers of beauty and of sanctity, bloom fragrant like my venture without cease.*

* Light three of the candles and let them burn. Then carry the picture outdoors, tip the petals off it, and repeat the words.

* Return indoors, light the last candle, tear a corner off the paper, burn it in the candle, drop it in the pot, rip the rest into small pieces, and bury the pieces and ash when the candle is burned.

CHAPTER 11

Becoming Rich and Famous and Making a Fortune Through Our Talents

Many of us dream of making our fortunes as movie or television stars, writing a bestselling book, appearing on a TV reality show or game program with huge prizes, being offered a major art or craft exhibition of our own, playing for a national or international team, or winning an Olympic medal. Dreams do come true, but sometimes not until later in life. Indeed, I didn't start writing until I was forty, a girl from the wrong side of the tracks, and now, at 71, I have published more than one hundred books. Of course, hard work is required to gain and sustain fame and fortune, but spells can open the channels to create the right opportunity in the right place and at the right time. Under the laws of manifesting action from thought and desires, a spell will help you to bring those dreams into actuality. Indeed, it is said that the more you believe your success will exceed your expectations, the easier your dreams will become reality.

A Goldstone Ritual to Attract Fame and Fortune

YOU WILL NEED

An orange glittery goldstone ✷ A small,
deep bowl almost filled with gold-colored coins and
gold foil stars ✷ A small, gold-colored bag

TIMING

Any evening before a competition or contest

THE SPELL

* Hold the goldstone in your writing hand while saying the following
  words three times, *Goldstone, grow luckier by the hour, increased shall
  you be in power and rich rewards upon me shower, make fame and fortune
  mine, so like you goldstone I shall shine.*

* Immerse the goldstone in the coins and stars, saying, *Fame and fortune
  shall be mine, I too, like gold, shall shine.*

* Leave the goldstone in the bowl.

* Whenever you go for an interview, audition, or performance, take the
  goldstone out of the bowl and carry it in the gold bag with some stars
  and coins.

* Return everything to the bowl until next time.

A Starry Night Spell to Make the Seemingly Impossible Possible

A place where you can see the stars clearly at
night, or stand under fairy or solar lights ✶ A blue and gold
lapis lazuli crystal or a large gold star (cut from gold foil)

TIMING

A starry night

THE SPELL

* Hold the crystal or star in your writing hand and look up at the stars while saying, *Star light, star bright, the first star I see tonight, I wish I may, I wish I might, have the wish I wish tonight.*

* Focus on one particular star, saying, *Star light, star bright, the first star I see tonight, let me rise to your heights, starry as the starry night.*

* Toss the crystal/star into the sky, saying, *I am starlight, I am star bright, I am the wish I wish tonight.*

* Walk away.

To Succeed in a Major Audition or Contest in Whatever Field You Choose

YOU WILL NEED

Two long, gold scarves or thick, long gold ribbons

TIMING

A windy day, or switch on a fan near the open front door

THE SPELL

* Tie one scarf/ribbon to the wrist of your non-writing hand and hold the second loosely in the other.

* Stand on the doorstep and, while facing outside, circle the scarves all around. Then go outdoors and turn in all directions while saying the following words faster and faster, *I am a star, I will go far, I will win great acclaim, soon all will know my name, for I am a star* [shout your name] *and I will go far.*

* Tie the scarves/ribbons to a nearby tree where they can blow free or go indoors and hang them from a high window facing the same direction as the front door.

To Succeed in a Major Sporting Competition

A T-shirt belonging to the desired team or sporting
event * A gold medallion on a chain

TIMING

Before the selection process or a step along the way

THE SPELL

* Put on the T-shirt and place the medallion around your neck, saying, *Dream seller, dream seller, bring to me fame, grant sporting success and increasing acclaim, bring my right place, so all know my face.*

* Start to sway, waving your arms over your head, saying, *Dream seller, dream seller, let me soon, let me rise, rise to the skies, win every prize.*

* Jump up and down, reaching upwards a little further each time; with a final leap, clasp your medal in your hands and say, *The prize is done, and I have won.*

* If possible, wear the T-shirt and medallion all day.

To Be Given a Place on and Win a Television Reality Show

YOU WILL NEED

Glitter pens and a large piece of
dark-colored paper * Glue

TIMING

Before applying to the show

THE SPELL

* Write the title of the show in glitter pens along the top of the paper. Underneath, write your name and the words, I AM THE WINNER AND I AM THE STAR, IN SUCH A SHORT TIME I HAVE COME VERY FAR, THE CAMERAS ARE FOCUSING ON ME, I AM THE WINNER OF THIS REALITY TV.

* In the center of the paper, stick pictures of previous winners and your picture in the center with the current year.

* Use different-colored pens to fill the paper with words such as, CONGRATULATIONS and A NEW STAR IS BORN.

* Hang the paper where light (such as a spot lamp) illuminates it.

To Be Offered a Prestigious Art Exhibition

178

YOU WILL NEED

A few of your paintings arranged along a wall
* A pointed clear quartz crystal * Six battery tealights
placed in a row on a surface in front of the paintings

TIMING

When you are seeking to exhibit or sell your work

THE SPELL

* Use the pointed tip of the crystal to gently touch each illuminated tealight in turn, left to right, while saying, *Light the way magically, point me to recognition that I may acclaim win and success through this exhibition.*

* Move the wand left to right in front of each painting, almost touching each with the wand, repeating the words.

* Leave the tealights burning for an hour, then retouch each light with the wand left to right while saying the words again.

* Switch off the tealights.

To Get a CEO Position or Rise High
in a Major Organization

YOU WILL NEED

Seven business-sized cards and a metallic pen
★ A hole punch and gold string ★ Seven clear quartz
or citrine crystals or seven pearls ★ A palm pot or
broad-leafed green plant (indoors or outdoors)

TIMING

The first seven days of the month

THE SPELL

* On day one (and using the metallic pen), write your business name and the title to which you aspire on each card. Say the following words each time, *I am pure gold, my successful future I behold, day by day, month by month, year by year, will it unfold.*

* Hang the first card on the palm plant with the gold string, and say, *Day by day and week by week, the top job I do seek.*

* Place the first crystal to start a circle around the palm in the soil.

* Each day for the following six days, repeat the spell.

To Make Big Money Through an Invention or a Totally Original Business Idea

YOU WILL NEED

A picture of your invention or a brief description of your idea
★ A box of small pearls or pearl buttons set on top of, and in the center of, the picture ★ A silver candle behind the picture

TIMING

Three nights before the full moon and the night of the full moon

THE SPELL

* Light the candle, saying, *Originality, ingenuity, brings recognition and plenteous money.*

* Take the box of pearls outdoors, raise it seven times to the moon, and say, *My invention/idea is a pearl, a money spinner, certain to be a total winner.*

* Return the pearls indoors and blow out the candle.

* Repeat the spell until the night of the full moon. On that night, leave the pearls outdoors all night and let the candle burn.

* Keep the pearls with the picture of the invention.

To Sell a Blockbuster Movie or Musical

A DVD of a bestselling movie or musical
* Six red roses * Six red ribbons

TIMING

The first day of the month

THE SPELL

* Bind the DVD with the red ribbons, saying, *A box office sensation, congratulations, a major hit, no doubt about it.*

* Pluck and scatter the rose petals on top of the DVD and then sprinkle them outdoors while saying, *An international winner, a crowded theatre/ cinema, fortune and fame, that's the game, in big lights my name.*

* Keep the ribbons tied around the DVD.

To Become an International Media Personality

YOU WILL NEED

A cheap, old drum (can be a child's) or a tambourine
* A box of gold and silver sequins * A semicircle
of gold candles or lamps around the drum

TIMING

After dark

THE SPELL

* Light the candles or lamps so light shines on the drum.

* Scatter sequins on top of the flat drum and begin shaking it gently
  from side to side, chanting, *I am on the cover of every glossy magazine,
  from flashing camera bulbs to silver shimmering screen, front page news
  quotes my views, the greatest star ever seen.*

* Keep rattling and chanting faster and faster and end with a final shake.

* Tip the sequins in a box and then glue them all over the cover of your
  favorite glossy magazine.

To Become a Millionaire Through Your Creative Talents

A long strip of white paper * Any bright
metallic pen * A frankincense incense stick

TIMING

Wednesday morning or waxing moon

THE SPELL

* Writing from the left, write a single number "1" and continue adding zeros and commas until you have gone across the page. As you're writing, say the following words continuously, *A millionaire, a billion, a trillionaire and more, keep adding noughts, just as I ought, until I have a zillion.*

* Light the incense. While holding it like a smoke pen, write in the air the number 1, then a zero, and keep adding smoke zeros while repeating the words continuously, until you reach the end of the paper.

* Leave the incense to burn through.

To Become an Overnight YouTube Sensation

The device on which you will upload your
music/production

TIMING

Sunday

THE SPELL

* Switch on the device and, depending on its size, sit or stand with your
  hands horizontal or vertical, palms outward, fingers together, an inch
  away from its screen, and repeat, *Views that run to millions, likes and
  comments by the zillions. I am a star, shooting so far, my profile extends
  through the world to its end, an overnight sensation, a new dazzling
  creation, m——eeeeeeeeeeeeeeeee, for all to see.*

* Sway and move your feet from side to side, your active hand
  circling clockwise and the other counterclockwise as you say the
  words rhythmically.

* When you feel ready, stamp and clap nine times, saying,
  I am a YouTube star and will go far.

* Upload your material.

To Attract a Life-Changing Opportunity
or to Attain Fame and Fortune

A small meteorite, obtainable from a crystal store or
online ☆ A red candle ☆ Magnetic sand (or ordinary
sand over which you have passed a magnet several times)
☆ A red drawstring bag ☆ Dried parsley or tarragon

TIMING

Tuesday night

THE SPELL

185

* Light the candle.

* Hold your meteorite up to the candlelight using your writing hand.
  While this is happening, say the following words three times, *Meteor
  with your fiery power and make this wish come true* [Name] *this hour, that
  I may blaze glorious as you.*

* Add the meteorite to the bag.

* Sprinkle magnetic sand and parsley into the bag, close and shake it three
  times, and repeat the words three more times.

* Leave the bag in front of the candle until the candle is burned.

* Carry the bag as a lucky charm, repeating the words and shaking the
  bag three times whenever a chance arises.

CHAPTER 12

Prosperity Through Compensation, Successful Redundancy OR Severance Packages, Insurance, AND Tax Claims

Sometimes things that may seem like setbacks can lead to financial advantages. A good redundancy or severance package can prepare you for a new business or job opportunity with an added financial boost. Insurance or compensation claims can free up money for future investment. And life-changing accidents or property damage caused by things like natural disasters can leave you with the funds to start something new. There are also many grants and government funds to help you convert your home into a more environmentally friendly place or provide a disabled relative with the care they need.

Spells are an excellent way of focusing psychic energies so that such financial boosts are more easily and swiftly realized. However, it's not uncommon to find that claims adjusters, tax officials, or those who administer official funds can prove unhelpful or even obstructive.

In this chapter, I focus on using magick to give impetus to resolving official disputes. The spells also address personal vendettas, those that perpetuate lies or deny just claims, and other obstacles to incoming funds. Some of the spells concentrate on bringing the truth to the light of day so that justice will be done. Such spells help relieve real financial hardship, whether that means surviving day-to-day or struggling to save for the future.

When You Are Fighting an Unjust Claim by the Taxation Department (IRS) to Deprive You of a Sizable Rebate

YOU WILL NEED

A triangle of three sandalwood incense sticks,
around a bowl of dried dill or thyme

TIMING

Thursday

THE SPELL

* Light the incense sticks clockwise, saying for each, *I call upon the power of Air, to redress this matter so unfair, all I ask is what I am due, and so again my plea renew.*

* Pass the first and second, then the first and third and the second and third incense sticks, one in each hand over the herbs so the ash drops in the bowl of herbs, saying, *The facts obscured, no longer endured, no more procrastinating shall there be, restore to me my rightful money.*

* When the incense is burned and the ash mix cooled, scatter the mix outdoors and vigorously pursue your claim.

When You Are Struggling for Financial Backing or Home or Workplace Modifications for a Disabled Relative or for Yourself

YOU WILL NEED

A closed padlock without a key ⋆ A brick wall
or wooden fence you can walk around ⋆ Green
plants or sunflower seeds

TIMING

After a setback

THE SPELL

* Hold the closed padlock saying, *You* [name authority or people blocking the improvements] *won't open the way to self-sufficiency at all, all you create continually is an insurmountable brick wall, now I say, now I see, the resources instantly shall be free.*

* Walk around the wall and bury or hide the padlock in soil or under stones on the other side.

* Plant green plants in the soil against the wall edge at the bottom or scatter seeds, saying, *Give me* [or name person struggling] *the means to make my own prosperity, knock down the wall/s, with the right resources I* [or name] *can achieve all.*

To Gain Fast Access to Retraining or Job Relocation if Your Organization or Industry is Threatened with Closure

YOU WILL NEED

A small blackboard or dark piece of slate
* White chalk

TIMING

Wednesday

THE SPELL

* On one side of the board, with the index finger of your active hand, draw an invisible door. On the same side of the board, invisibly draw (again with your index finger) the words, OLD DOOR CLOSING.

* Throw water on the board and leave it to dry, saying, *Wash away the doubts and fears, the message I give the world is clear, no becomes yes, I can't I can, and so a springboard I demand.*

* Draw a white open chalk door on top of the invisible one and say, *A new, more prosperous future than before, I walk through opportunity's opening door.*

* Apply for retraining as well as for new positions in your declining job field in ever-widening geographical areas.

For a Good Redundancy or Severance Package if Your Job is Disappearing After Many Years

YOU WILL NEED

A box of silver-colored pins, preferably pearl-tipped, the kind used in crafts ⋆ A velvet pincushion ⋆ A gold pendant or medallion ⋆ A gold candle behind the pincushion

TIMING

Waning moon

THE SPELL

* Place the pincushion with the pendant or medallion in the center and the box of pins to the right.

* Light the candle. Stick the pins in clockwise widening circles into the cushion around the medallion while saying, *Not empty handed, but well-rewarded, given acclaim so I may start again, either in employment or business in my own name.*

* When you have used all the pins, put on the medallion, saying, *Well rewarded even though not sought, a good package I gain to take me forward.*

* Let the candle burn.

* Keep the cushion with your severance documents.

* Wear the medallion.

To Make Sure You Avoid Any Large-Scale Threatened Dismissals at Work

YOU WILL NEED

A dead crumbling twig * A branch on a tree or
bush with growing leaves * Any small, decorative
party flags or Buddhist banner flags

TIMING

Saturday or waning moon

THE SPELL ·

* Sit outdoors where there is soil, preferably in a high place.

* Crumble the dead stick, saying, *Dead wood is there plenty, my workplace needs to empty, to improve profitability and efficiency, but this definitely does not or will not affect me.*

* Drape the party flags or Buddhist banner flags over the thriving tree branch, saying, *My job remains alive, in the new order I will thrive, changes will benefit me, and better prospects shall I see.*

* Bury the dead wood and let the wind carry the banner away on its own time.

If You Have Made a Financial or Administrative Error and Are Being Threatened with Official Action

YOU WILL NEED

A piece of grey paper ★ A soft grey lead pencil ★ An eraser or eraser fluid

TIMING

Just before sunset

THE SPELL

* In the dimming light, write (lightly) in pencil, AN UNINTENTIONAL ERROR WAS MADE, BUT I CAN PUT IT RIGHT, LET THE CONSEQUENCES OF MY ACTION/OVERSIGHT, FADE WITH THE DISAPPEARING LIGHT.

* As the light fades, rub out the words on the paper, starting with the last letter and going backwards, ending on the first letter. While doing this, say, *Undone, erased, with the dying light, so do all bad consequences fade from sight.*

* Shred the paper and dispose of it in an outside trash can or flush it away down the toilet.

To Overturn a Rejected Insurance or Compensation Claim That, Unless Settled, Will Seriously Affect Your Future Prosperity

YOU WILL NEED

Children's play sand in a tray * A sand
bucket * A children's spade

TIMING

Sunday

THE SPELL

* Fill the bucket with sand and tap the sand down. Then turn it over and pat on top of the inverted bucket ten times while saying the following words ten times, *Overturn this wrong decision, override this bad conclusion, the claim is just and cannot be denied, behind legal jargon you* [name company] *can no longer hide.*

* Tip over the sandcastle. Around it, build up sand walls and decorate the structure with shells, stones, or tiny clear crystal chippings while saying, *Building up the evidence, the truth is shining bright, overturn the wrong and bring justice to light.*

* Flatten it all and write with the spade in the sand, JUSTICE SHALL BE DONE, ALL SHALL BE RIGHT

To Receive Adequate Compensation When You Have Been Unfairly Treated or Dismissed

YOU WILL NEED

A small, sealed canister of rice

TIMING

At sunrise

THE SPELL

* Bang the canister lid ten times while saying the following words ten times, *Half a pound of fifty cent rice, accept it I'm not able, nor willing to even consider the offer you've put on the table.*

* Bang ten more times saying, *Up your paltry offer instantly, after all my effort, efficiency, do you think I'm a charity?*

* Bang ten more times, saying, *So as soon as you are able, please return to the negotiating table, and I will go peacefully, when you offer realistically.*

* Make a final bang and say, *Sooner you start talking, sooner I'll be walking.*

* Keep the canister in the kitchen and bang on it each morning while saying the final spell words. Do this until everything is settled.

To Obtain Sufficient Compensation if You Have Suffered a Life-Changing Injury When Those Responsible Are Denying Liability

YOU WILL NEED

A deep bowl filled with different-colored feathers
(obtainable from a party or craft store)

TIMING

Any windy day outdoors

THE SPELL

* Run your fingers through the feathers (don't worry if they start blowing away) while saying the following words continuously, *Soften the loss, ease the blow, compensation will help my life regrow, not as before yet there can be more.*

* Start blowing the feathers gently from the top of the bowl so they fly free, saying between breaths, *Take responsibility, admit liability, no denials, no excuse, this is too important to refuse.*

* Tip out the final feathers while saying the amount you need and the following words, *No delay, I ask not for retribution, only you pay, my life cannot be as before, but there can be more.*

If an Insurance Company, Landlord, or Corporation is Dragging Its Heels Over an Urgent Property or Building Defect or After a Natural Disaster

YOU WILL NEED

A metal sieve ⋆ Flour that won't go through
the holes ⋆ A jug of water

TIMING

Saturday

THE SPELL

* Pour the water into the sieve, saying, *Words on deaf ears never stay, like water always draining away, a new excuse, a hidden clause, living with the consequences of yet another pause.*

* Dry the sieve and pour flour into it until it is nearly full, then clatter it on a hard surface seven times while saying the following words seven times, *A watertight case, full payment within seven days, the end of delays, is that clear? This you shall hear.*

* Make a final clatter and use the flour to make a celebration cake.

* Bombard the offenders mercilessly with final demands.

If Your Business Reputation Has Been Damaged by a False Accusation or Attempts to Close You Down

YOU WILL NEED

Sour grapes on a stalk ⋆ Vinegar
⋆ Nine lemon seeds ⋆ Bitter aloes
(optional) ⋆ A waterproof container

TIMING

New moon, before the crescent moon appears

THE SPELL

* Pluck the grapes one by one and drop them into the container saying, *Sour grapes, spite and lies, your undeserved viciousness I despise.*

* Add the lemon seeds and, if using them, bitter aloes. While doing this, say, *Sharp and sour indeed, but this unfairness will I stop with speed.*

* Add just a little vinegar to cover the fruit and say, *So your viciousness shall I freeze, then all your attacks against me cease.*

* Put on the lid and place the container into the coldest part of the freezer (vinegar freezes at 28 degrees Fahrenheit and not 32 degrees Fahrenheit, as water does).

* Leave it in the freezer and take swift action.

If You Are Being Unfairly Sued for a Liability or Situation That You Know is False

A lemon ★ A hand juicer ★ A bowl of clear
water placed beneath the juicer

TIMING

Thursday

THE SPELL

* Hold the lemon in both hands saying, *Innocent am I free, from stain,
  all your accusations false remain, you* [Name] *seek only to profit from me,
  I send back with contempt, what is ill-meant, I reject your infamy.*

* Squeeze the lemon so the juice falls into the water and say, *So do I wash
  away, all untrue claims, with which my life you do defame, these unjust
  charges shall not stay, but fade into the truth of day.*

* Discard the flesh and say, *Withdraw your lies or justice will your falsehoods
  deride, I fear you not, only despise.*

* Wash the lemon water away under flowing water.

If You Are Applying for a Major Enterprise or Improvement Grant but Suspect There is Corruption Behind the Scenes

YOU WILL NEED

Dough or children's play clay ⋆ A rolling pin
⋆ Twelve small, white stones or crystals ⋆ Twelve
small, red stones or crystals

TIMING

Waning moon

THE SPELL

* Roll out the dough/clay so that there is an uneven surface and it slopes upwards. Press the red stones unevenly across it. Say, *An uneven playing field methinks, obstacles and pitfalls waiting, were all things even I should win, but fairness there is missing.*

* Remove the red stones and roll out the clay/dough so it is level and say, *No hidden agenda or prior deals, palm greasing nor whispered appeals.*

* Make a pathway of white stones from one side of the dough/clay to the other and say, *Equality is the name of the game, we all start and finish the same.*

* Cast the red stones into water.

CHAPTER 13

Dealing with Financial Disputes Involving Emotions, such as Divorces, Inheritances, and Family Property Disagreements

F ighting for your financial freedom becomes harder when loved ones turn against you, whether it is due to divorce or an inheritance. The latter is made all the more painful when we may have been the one to care for a now-deceased person in their lifetime, often at great financial sacrifice, only to be threatened with being turned out of our only home. Sadly, children can be used by one party in marital breakups as financial pawns and levers to extract maximum financial advantage and for that party to pay as little as possible over many years.

Family property, too, especially if involving a business where the whole family and their partners and children are involved, can be a blessing but become a burden if one person wants to leave or start a new venture. Lack of confidence, as well as actual power by the one controlling the finances, can create a sense of helplessness. Because magick is strengthened by emotion, family financial disputes while doubly painful are especially susceptible to positive magick, both to provide protection against intimidation or major guilt-tripping and to give courage to stand for what you want at a time when you are extra-emotionally vulnerable. I have created most of these spells specifically for clients. They're meant to address many common financial problems and crises.

Cheating Ex-Partner Who is Hiding Assets to Avoid a Fair Settlement

YOU WILL NEED

A steamed-up bathroom mirror
* A white cloth

TIMING

Any waxing moon morning

THE SPELL

* Push your hands, palms vertical, toward the steamed-up mirror and say, *The future I cannot clearly see, but I know you are deceiving me, bring to this settlement clarity, for you hide to the world your dishonesty.*

* Write the same words in the steam.

* Then breathe on the mirror three times, saying between breaths, *I will have clarity financially.*

* Rub the mirror counterclockwise with the cloth while saying, *Remove obscurity, deception, and secrecy* until the mirror is clear.

* Open the window and door and say, *In the light of day, all deception will blow away.*

* Repeat the spell before any major negotiations.

If Your Ex-Partner is Bullying or Intimidating You to Settle for Less Than Your Rights but Pretending Cooperation to the World

Twelve sharp, silver pins placed in a wheel formation, sharp ends inwards ★ A picture of your ex-partner placed inside the wheel ★ A thick piece of bubble wrap ★ Strong adhesive tape

TIMING

The end of the waning moon

THE SPELL

* Touch the blunt end of each pin in turn clockwise, saying for each, *Sharp, sharp, though publicly you smile and with your wiles, nice guy/gal, do play, you treat me with derision and bully me into submission, but no more shall you have your way.*

* Enclose the picture and pins tightly in the bubble wrap and tape it securely, saying, *Your viciousness is bound. I won't have you around.*

* Dump the parcel in a garbage can away from your home.

If Your Ex-Partner is Using the Children as Pawns to Deprive You and the Family of a Fair Financial Settlement and Property Following a Breakup

YOU WILL NEED

A pawn from a chess set for each of the children, placed in front of a white candle to represent your joint financial assets * A king and/or queen for you and your ex, placed on either side of the candle * A shredder or sharp chopping knife * Two paper bags

TIMING

Before sunset

THE SPELL

* Light the assets candle, saying, *No longer use the children as your pawns, pieces in your game, treat them as vulnerable souls, not assets to be claimed.*

* Remove the pawns from the candle, saying, *Checkmate, I end this stalemate, separate fairly, without enmity, reality, not chess, no more, no less.*

* When the assets candle is burned through and cooled, shred it and divide it between the two paper bags, with the queen in one and the king in the other. Keep the bags sealed until everything is settled.

When You Discover a Close Family Member in the Business Has Been Siphoning Off Assets for Years

YOU WILL NEED

A picture on the computer of both of you together

TIMING

As soon as you discover the asset thefts

THE SPELL

* Hover the cursor over each of you in turn saying, *I thought business and family were the perfect fix, now I find they do not mix.*

* Create a thick vertical line between the two of you on the screen and say, *Though right now none believes me, no more shall your deception be against the interests of the family.*

* Print out a reduced image of the thief and say, *Damage limitation, from your cheating ways I you separate, though ties of family still penetrate.*

* Bind the image with three knots of red thread and hide it in the workplace while saying, *I bind your trickery, until the time you can go, then your dealings all shall know.*

* When you have evidence, burn the knots and image.

If a Family Member You Cared for Died Without Leaving a Will and Other Relatives Want to Make You Homeless

A piece of white paper on which you have drawn a blue square to represent the home ★ Yellow jasper placed around the outside of the square, one for each person trying to take your home away ★ Lemongrass oil placed in a burner ★ A yellow bag

TIMING

Full moon

209

THE SPELL

* Light the oil and pass each jasper in turn through the steam, naming each person. Then say, *Where were you in the hard times? I gave up all, never once did you answer my call.*

* Blow out the oil candle and tie the crystals in a yellow bag outside the square, saying, *Time in the future, for claiming your share, when you were needed, you simply weren't there.*

* Leave the bag with things to be organized in the house.

If a Formerly Happy Family is Being Ripped Apart by an Inheritance Dispute

YOU WILL NEED

A silk scarf or cloth ⋆ Poppy seeds ⋆ A small, dark
stone or crystal for each difficult family member
and a small, white stone for each supportive
member (include yourself in this)

TIMING

Friday

THE SPELL

* Place the stones on the scarf in two clusters. Scatter poppy seeds on top of the stones saying, *We are one family, our* [name deceased relative] *always kept peace, now is the time for dissension to cease.*

* Draw together the corners of the scarf and secure them with three knots so that everything remains within.

* Open the cloth outdoors and scatter the contents while saying, *We are one family, disputes and bitterness cannot be, let us find peaceful resolution, love is the inheritance and love the conclusion.*

* Send a reconciliation note and flowers to everyone involved, no matter how undeserving.

If There is Division Over a Deceased Relative's Jewelry and Possessions

YOU WILL NEED

Crystals in any color, one for each family member involved
* A photo of the deceased person, placed next to the deceased person's favorite flowers and the crystals * A white candle

TIMING

Friday

THE SPELL

* Surround the photo and flowers with a circle of crystals, touching and naming a person for each crystal. Say, *We are here circled in unity, quarrelling was not what* [name deceased person] *intended to be, can we not share mutually in* [Name]'*s beloved memory?*

* Pass your hands, your active hand clockwise and the other counterclockwise, over the photo, the crystal circle, and the flowers while repeating the words softly.

* Light the candle and leave it to burn.

* Afterward, send a copy of the photo and the person's crystal with a note suggesting you all meet for a memory day and share the possessions amicably.

211

If You Have Inherited Money or an Unexpected Family Gift and Want to Fulfill a Dream, but Others Say You Should Save It for a Rainy Day

YOU WILL NEED

A dream catcher with lots of feathers
hanging from it ★ Scissors

TIMING

Wednesday at sunrise

THE SPELL

* Hang your dream catcher where the breeze catches it and swing it gently, saying, *Dreams become possibility, my dreams can come true, let me not listen to should or ought, but follow fulfillment anew.*

* Cut off a few feathers and set them free outdoors, saying, *Prosperity is not just money saved, but abundance to be explored, fortunes are made through being brave and walking through life's door.*

* Finally, cut off a crystal from your dream catcher and keep it with you as a talisman as you plan your adventure and seek limitless fortune and fulfillment.

* Leave the dream catcher for when you return.

If You Are Pressured into Giving Up Equity or Savings in Order to Assist a Younger Family Member Who Never Pays Back

YOU WILL NEED

Two bags or purses, one blue, one red ∗ A bowl of coins placed between them ∗ A red candle and a blue candle

TIMING

Before a visit

THE SPELL

∗ Shake the coins, saying, *I have scrimped and saved, slogged and slaved then along you waltz* [name relative] *with your grandiose plans at my expense, full of dreams and no common sense.*

∗ Light the red candle and put the coins in the red bag and shake it, saying, *All for you, little for me, taking all my equity, for dividends I'll never see.*

∗ Light the blue candle and tip the coins into your blue bag from the red one, saying, *You are young, make your own light, mine cannot grow dim as yours grows bright.*

∗ Leave both candles to burn.

If Your Financial Future and Freedom Are Being Held Back Because You Are Tied to a Family Property, Land, or Business

YOU WILL NEED

A brown clay figure for each significant person, including yourself ★ Brown cord or strong thread ★ A heatproof bowl half filled with sand ★ Scissors

TIMING

Crescent moon

THE SPELL

* Wrap all the figures tightly in the cords and knot them together so they are tangled. Say *I am bound unwillingly to this business/property that you say will one day belong to me, but I have dreams of my own, this family venture/property I have outgrown.*

* Snip the figures free from the cords, saying, *I cut not family devotion or loyalty, but seek to free myself financially, that I may my own person be, and make the fortune right for me.*

* Drop the cut cords into the bowl and set fire to them.

If Because of Your Culture or Religion Your Future Marriage is Tied to Family Financial Arrangements

YOU WILL NEED

Two gold chain necklaces, each slightly too tight to wear   *   Four nag champa-fragrance incense cones set in a square   *   A rose quartz heart on a small ring or loop

TIMING

Friday before sunset

215

THE SPELL

* Light the incense cones and pass the first chain and then the second chain separately through the smoke of each cone clockwise while saying, *Too tight, too restrictive, I respect my family, yet in love must I be free.*

* Open the chains and pass both together through the incense smoke.

* Attach the rose quartz to one chain. Fasten the chains together to make a single large chain. Then say, *I will marry for love alone, I am not a pawn of wealth, I will make my own fortune and choose my bride/groom myself.*

* Find a sympathetic friend or mentor to help you negotiate.

If An Elderly Relative is Holding You to Ransom Financially and Emotionally with the Promise of a Future Inheritance

A small, heavy grey pillar-shaped stone
★ A white pumice stone

TIMING

Waning moon

THE SPELL

* Set the pillar-shaped stone on the ground outdoors, surrounded by space.

* Say, *You* [name relative] *promise me riches if my life I put on hold, I fear to lose all, so I do as I am told.*

* Hold the pumice stone and say, *Though I fear being cast adrift, yet I shall make my way by my own gifts, become light as air as my spirit lifts.*

* Throw the pumice stone as far as you can past the pillar-shaped stone and say, *And so I walk, afraid but free, shedding off threats of poverty, and my own wealth I'll draw to me.*

* Collect your pumice stone and keep it as a talisman whenever you waver.

If You Want to Move on From a Friend's Business but Are Being Made to Feel Guilty and Responsible for Its Survival

YOU WILL NEED

An open space ✴ A complete circle of stones
large enough for you to stand in ✴ Flower petals
in a basket placed in the circle center

TIMING

The day before a crescent moon

THE SPELL

* Walk around the inside of the circle counterclockwise, saying,
  You [name business partner], *I keep you afloat day by day, no wonder you don't want me to move away, in the prison of obligation you leave no door, acting the victim, but I see the score.*

* Dismantle the circle clockwise, leaving the stones in a neat pile to form a doorway in the now-invisible circle.

* Now make a circle of flowers or seeds over the same space. They should be able to blow away, leaving only the stone doorway.

If Your Wealthy In-Laws Control Your Partner with Money

A box filled with coins ∗ A brown cord tied around
the box, with the two ends of the cord
hanging on either side of the box

TIMING

The first of the month

THE SPELL

* Pull the box toward you by one of the dangling cords, saying,
  Tug of war for [name partner]*'s emotions, tow the line, another bribe
  and all is fine.*

* Pull the box toward you by the other dangling cord, saying, *What do
  I offer in exchange for gold, love, commitment, loyalty untold, yet you waver
  time and time again, to give them pleasure you cause me pain.*

* Undo the cord gently and carefully, saying, *I release the ties of emotional
  blackmail, love over money shall prevail.*

* Burn the cord. Leave the box of coins near your in-laws' home and make
  plans to move much farther away from the in-laws.

If You Are a Constant Piggy Bank for Your Adult Children and See Your Retirement Ever Receding

YOU WILL NEED
A piggy bank

TIMING
After the latest demand

THE SPELL

* Shake your piggy bank five times, saying, *Piggy bank, piggy bank, my security does not stay, my retirement fund constantly diminishes, with their extravagant desires and wishes, piggy bank hide my money away.*

* Shake your piggy bank five time more, saying, *A coin in, four coins out and there is never enough, to satisfy all their needs, they say please, I say yes, they ask for more, and to my distress, hey presto I have less.*

* Hide your piggy bank, saying, *Out of sight if not of mind, and so I must say no, you're nice to me when you have need, this is not love but blatant greed, so to your bank please go.*

CHAPTER 14

Saving Money
IN THE Long AND
Short Term

Throughout this book, there have been a variety of spells for growing money, including using money plants such as basil, under which coins were buried. The accumulation of wealth where more comes in than goes out underpins the principles of prosperity magick.

This chapter focuses on spells to make savings grow faster, whether the money is for a home, a first car, or a trip later in life. There can be many threats to your savings, including unexpected expenses, domestic crises, or the ongoing needs of children of every age. Savings too can be a source of friction in relationships, especially when one partner saves and the other spends extravagantly on trivialities or addictive habits, such as gambling or alcohol.

So, too, can savings be eaten up if retirement funds or redundancy payments and pensions don't plan out the way we'd hoped. What should have been a time of ease seems to transform into working forever just to keep afloat. Finally, especially in the later years of a relationship, there can be serious disputes about how to spend lifetime savings, with one partner wanting to hang on to every dollar and the other wanting to live life to the fullest. In short, savings are critical, as they are an investment in our own happiness and dreams.

Cosmic Bargaining if You Seem to be Giving More to Life in Effort Than You're Getting Back Economically

223

YOU WILL NEED

Seven plain cards, the size of playing cards ✳ A red pen

TIMING

Sunday

THE SPELL

✳ On one side of each card write GIVE and on the other side write TAKE.

✳ Shuffle the cards and say the following words quickly, *Give and take, I give my all, scrimp and save, two steps forward one step back, Cosmos, you surely fairness lack.*

✳ Flip the cards one on top of the other, saying, *Redress the balance, Cosmos, let me get ahead, I work hard, please flip the cards, so I win instead.*

✳ Turn all the cards so TAKE is uppermost and say, *Do give me the means to live for the hard work I daily give and best of all what I crave, some to save.*

✳ Carry a different card with you, with TAKE uppermost each day.

A Russian Golden Flower Spell Ritual to Increase Your Savings Capacity from New Sources in the Year Ahead

YOU WILL NEED

A small, slightly dry yellow flower (best of all golden-colored dried fern)

TIMING

Midsummer's Eve June 23, or any Sunday sunset

THE SPELL

* Holding your golden flower, climb a hill or stand in an open place as the sun is setting.

* Break off the petals and cast them towards the sunset, saying, *Golden flower/fern bring to me, savings increasing steadily, that my fortunes may in the year ahead accumulate and stay secure, golden flower/fern may my fortunes like you remain golden and endure.*

* Take a small quantity of the flower home and keep it in a sachet with your savings receipts or certificates or near your computer for online transactions.

* Replace it the following Midsummer's Eve or after a year.

Another Midsummer Savings Ritual to Guide You to the Best Options and Opportunities to Save Money

As many golden-colored seeds such as gold linseed, gold flax, or striped sunflower seeds as there are days in the coming month (if Midsummer's Eve, start from then and include the whole following month of July) ✳ A tall tin or jar with a lid ✳ Any large area of earth, preferably unplanted

TIMING

Midsummer's Eve, or the first day of any month, early

THE SPELL

✳ Put your seeds in the tin or jar and seal the lid.

✳ When you reach the open space, shake the tin the number of times there are seeds inside and say the following words before you begin, *Savings increase and multiply, good options and opportunities intensify, into my life pop and fly.*

✳ Take off the lid and walk, scattering seeds until they are all gone.

To Rapidly Increase Your Savings in a Major Push Towards a Dream

YOU WILL NEED

A new banknote, a second worth double the first,
and a third worth at least double the second
* A white resealable envelope * Dried parsley,
sage, and thyme mixed herbs * A blue pen

TIMING

Two consecutive nights

THE SPELL

* Put the smallest value banknote in the envelope and write the following phrase on the envelope, DOUBLE MY SAVINGS, THE RIGHT FACTORS MIX, DOUBLE MY MONEY, THIS SHALL I FIX.

* Put it on the table.

* Sprinkle the herb mix around the envelope while saying the same words.

* Leave overnight. Next night, add the second bank note to the envelope and reseal it while saying, *Triple my savings, ever increase, triple the money, may this never cease.*

* Place on the table and scatter two more herb circles over the first, repeating all the spell words fast.

* Next morning, sweep up the herbs and cast them outdoors.

A Traditional All-Purpose Money-Incubating Ritual

A brown pottery jar with a lid * A green candle
* Ongoing coins, starting with one you were given
* A jar of sunflower seeds (top up regularly)

TIMING

Every morning

THE SPELL

* Open the pot and, holding a coin in your hands, say, *May my savings daily grow, money inwards flow, enough for pleasure and some treasure and a rainy day.*

* Drop the coin into the pot, put on the lid, and blow out the candle.

* Scatter some seeds outdoors, saying, *Savings expand on every hand, over sea and over land, accumulating in my pot, start with a little, end with a lot.*

* Leave the pot in a warm place indoors, such as the kitchen, and each day repeat the spell.

* When your pot is full, add the coins to your savings, but leave one in the pot.

The Ultimate Piggy Bank Spell

YOU WILL NEED

A china piggy bank * An odd number of coins,
given to you in change before the day of the spell
* A green candle * A yellow citrine crystal

TIMING

Wednesday

THE SPELL

* Light the candle and add the citrine and two coins to the piggy bank to make an odd number to be increased. Then say, *Accumulate, make more, with savings fill, and soon the pig will money spill.*

* Shake the pig three times, repeating the words.

* Wish for the total amount you will need and blow out the candle.

* Light the candle whenever you put money in, repeating the spell.

* When the piggy bank is full, transfer your savings, but always leave in the citrine and two coins.

* When you have reached your goal, empty and smash the pig. Replace it and add the citrine and two coins to the new one and set a new goal.

A Twelve-Month Savings Plan for Your First Home, Car, or Major Purchase When It Seems an Impossible Dream to Attain

A gold-colored dish ✳ A small gold item
✳ Eleven more small golden items
✳ A lidded box in which to keep the items

TIMING

The beginning of each month at noon

THE SPELL

✳ Set the gold dish to catch the light.

✳ Add the personal gold item, saying, *From modest beginnings does great fortune grow, this* [name purpose of savings] *is closer than it seems, month by month more savings show, and within the year it shall be so.*

✳ Hold up the dish to the light and repeat the words.

✳ As soon as possible, make a monthly deposit and keep the receipt under the dish.

✳ On the first day of each month, add a gold item to the dish, until you attain your goal.

If Your Partner Wastes Money on Luxuries and Trivialities and You Desperately Need to Save

YOU WILL NEED

A small, flat, heavy white stone ∗ A small piece of iron pyrites
or fool's gold or grey shining hematite ∗ White chalk

TIMING

Waning moon

THE SPELL

∗ While standing near your hearth or stove, hold up the pyrites and say,
All that glitters is not gold, but money buys for you [name partner]
*all that you behold, I try to save, you fritter away, there will be
nothing left for a rainy day.*

∗ Tape the pyrites under the doormat or hide them under the doorstep.

∗ On the base of the white stone, chalk your partner's name and say,
*This will surely weigh you down, stop you being the financial clown.
Henceforward money will not on toys be poured away, but as
solid savings in my hands will stay.*

∗ Keep the stone, chalk-side hidden, near the front door.

If Your Partner is Thrifty and Won't Use Hard-Earned Savings for Pleasure or to Fulfill Dreams

YOU WILL NEED

An old, battered wallet or purse * Sewing thread
tied or roughly sewn around it * Scissors

TIMING

Crescent moon

THE SPELL

* Hold the wallet, saying, *Tight as a proverbial tick, all these years I've saved for adventure, now you will hardly venture, much beyond the TV screen, it wasn't for this I worked for the dream.*

* Cut or rip open the wallet and take it outdoors, shaking it in the air, saying, *Moths fly away, too long in there have you slumbered and stayed, now fresh air is blowing through and I am off to pastures new.*

* Dump the wallet and thread and propose a major trip paid for from the savings, declaring you will go alone if necessary—and meaning it.

If Your Partner is Secretive About Savings and You Suspect There is a Hidden Cache

YOU WILL NEED

A wooden or ceramic fairy door ⋆ In front of it, a row of hazelnuts ⋆ Behind it, a closed bag containing cotton wool and coins ⋆ A long twig with a small, forked branch on the end

TIMING

A dark night

THE SPELL

* Touch each of the nuts in turn, saying, *All very innocent, all above board, this is all we have my dear, all we can afford.*

* Poke your stick through the fairy door saying, *Fairy tales are for children, and you have spun me one, let's see what you're hiding here, at last I've done my sums.*

* Hook the bag on the other side of the door and bring it through the door, adding the nuts.

* Get together facts and figures and make a joint appointment with your financial adviser.

A Major Family Economy Drive
to Balance the Books

A new broom and a new white duster

Crescent moon

* Flick your duster over any light switches often left on, any offending
  taps frequently left running, or any other areas of waste, and say, *New
  broom, new times, savings to be made, wastage is no longer fine, I'm finally
  drawing the line.*

* When you've finished, shake the duster out the front door.

* Sweep in counterclockwise circles through every room, ending at the
  front door. Brush any dust out the front door, then stand the broom
  bristles-end upwards.

* Go indoors and close the door firmly while saying, *New broom, new
  regime, be more careful with my money, gone are the days of milk and honey,
  the new rules please see.*

* Hang a list of economies in the kitchen. Point it out to family members,
  with monetary fines for infringements.

233

If You're Saving for a Major Purchase or Life Change but Feel Life is Passing You By

YOU WILL NEED

Six eggs in a bowl ✻ A small basket filled
with flowers and greenery

TIMING

Sunday

THE SPELL

✻ Hold the bowl of eggs, saying, *All our/my eggs in one basket, waiting for them to hatch, saving sensibly, living economically, so worthwhile, but when did we/I last smile?*

✻ Take one of the eggs and put it in the flower-filled basket, saying, *We/I get ever closer to the dream, but life passes us/me by, it seems. A little fun, a little lightness, today we/I really need to play.*

✻ Float the sixth egg in the basket on water, saying, *And afterwards we/I will go on beavering away, but first we/I must enjoy this day.*

✻ Have fun and build in occasional breaks in frugality.

If The Savings Won't Go as Far as You Hoped Because of Pension Shortfalls or Drops in Housing Prices

YOU WILL NEED

A box of children's bricks

TIMING

Saturday

THE SPELL

* Make a wall as high as possible with the bricks. If there aren't enough to make a long wall, reduce the height. While building the wall, say, *Not what we hoped and yet can we, make things go further with ingenuity.*

* Pass your hands over the wall in circles. Your writing hand should move clockwise, while the other hand should move counterclockwise. While doing this, say the following words continuously, *Make all go further, find new income sources, new resources, modify our plans, downsize a little, quality of a slightly different life attain, turn our loss into gain.*

* Use the brick box to add to the wall, saying, *Come to us creativity, let us see new opportunity and happy we shall be and free.*

* Start replanning, and new opportunities will come.

CHAPTER 15

Overcoming Debt, Unscrupulous Moneylenders, AND Debt Collectors; Stopping Money FROM Flowing Out Faster Than It Comes In

For a considerable number of people, the road to prosperity is slowed by the reality of money flowing out faster than it comes in. I have included spells to help shopaholics or people with partners who drain the household budget or have addictions to alcohol, gambling, or drugs.

Problems with debt occur among many responsible people. Borrowings can escalate due to caring for young children, paying for clothes, or being taken advantage of by loan sharks. Although there are conventional methods of help, including charities and debt assistance programs, spells include positive energies that can be useful when there are no resolutions in sight.

Spells can also give you the power and confidence to act decisively and stand up to financial bullies at a time when people are making you feel powerless. Above all, they can call and regenerate new moneymaking opportunities, sources, and resources to slowly turn the outflow into inflow. Even if you have been made bankrupt or filed for bankruptcy as a last resort, spells can give you the energy and impetus to start again in a new, more dynamic way.

An All-Purpose Anti-Debt Ritual
If You Have Been Made to Feel
Powerless or Worthless

YOU WILL NEED

Two pieces of slate (use roof slating)
* White chalk * An eraser

TIMING

Tuesday

THE SPELL

* Write on one slate, BANISH DEBT, and while holding it between your hands, say, *Debt, debt go away, you daily do my life dismay, I wipe you out, I get on top, debt, debt you must stop.*

* Smash the slate and dispose of it, and on the other slate write SOLVENCY and leave it in sunlight.

* Renew the word whenever it fades.

Clearing Away the Cobwebs of Debt

An abandoned indoor spiderweb or one in an
outhouse or on the side of a building ∗ A long
broom or feather duster ∗ Gold thread

TIMING

Saturday in sunlight

THE SPELL

∗ Carefully, and after asking permission of the vacating spider, unthread
the web using the broom/duster. Shake the cobweb off the broom/duster
outdoors (make sure all of it is gone) and say, *Old debt, old chaos, your
tangles I unbind, old web, redundant web, you I unwind, and so in clearing
dust, find the way I must, the thread of solvency, shall come to me.*

∗ Hold the broom/duster up to the light and weave gold threads
through it.

∗ Leave bristles or feathers up outdoors until nightfall

∗ Go tackle the most pressing financial problem.

To Stop Money Flowing Out of Your Life Faster Than It Flows In

YOU WILL NEED

A jug of water * A lidded, plastic container * Patchouli essential oil, traditionally called liquid gold

TIMING

Three days before the full moon

THE SPELL

* Fill up the jug and tip out half the water, then stop and say, *Money no longer flow away, you must stay, first to hold, then expand, then turn to gold.*

* Freeze the rest of the water in the container in the coldest part of the freezer for three days.

* On the night of the full moon, let it melt and add a few drops of patchouli oil. Swirl the mixture around while saying, *Stopped is the outflow, may gold grow.*

* Keep your liquid gold in a small orange or amber-colored glass dish until the next evening, then add more patchouli and burn the mixture in an oil burner or diffuser.

A Moon Month Candle Ritual to Reduce Spiraling Debt

YOU WILL NEED

A blue tealight for every day from full moon night to the following full moon night, placed in a circle ★ A paper in the center, divided into squares, one for each night of the moon month ahead (twenty-eight or twenty-nine) ★ Scissors

TIMING

The moon month, check online for length

THE SPELL

* On night one, write in each square, *Debt diminish soon by the next moon.*

* Light all of the tealights, repeating the words.

* Blow out the lights, cut off the first square, and burn it.

* Each night light one fewer candle and cut off and burn one more square.

* By the night of the next full moon, light the final unlit candle, then relight the others and leave them to burn.

* Afterwards, burn the final square saying, *May all be resolved by the power of the moon.*

Stopping the Drain of Debt

YOU WILL NEED

A sieve ✶ A saucepan of similar size, with a lid
✶ A favorite food you can simmer or steam in water

TIMING

Sunday

THE SPELL

✶ Hold the sieve under a running tap and let water run through it, saying,
*Water through a sieve, something soon must give, to hold on to my resources,
I need money from new sources.*

✶ Replace the sieve with the saucepan and partly fill it with water, saying,
*Money put to better use, flowing not away, but building up security, stability
now shall stay.*

✶ Add your favorite uncooked food to the saucepan, put on the lid, and
gently simmer the pot, saying, *Building up again, loss shall turn to gain,
purpose returns, my fortunes turn.*

✶ As you eat the food, picture money being abso[rbed]
through new opportunities.

If You Are Being Threatened by a Particularly Nasty Debt Collector or Debt-Collecting Company and the Law Won't Help

YOU WILL NEED

A twisted stick * Red paint and brush
or a permanent marker pen

TIMING

After a nasty phone call or visit

THE SPELL

* On the stick, draw or paint eyes and a serpent's tongue and mark the tail.

* Twist it between your hands saying, *Your power to hurt, I take away from this hour, your subtle sting, no more will bring me pain, I spit your venom back to you, send it not again.*

* Forget what your mother told you about good manners just for a moment. Spit on the twig, sprinkle it with sugar, and leave it near an ant's nest.

* Horrid? Not really. You are just returning the venom and assisting other vulnerable souls, for you can be sure you are not the only victim.

If Addiction by a Partner or Family Member is Ruining Your Finances

A small, insulated box ✳ Bubble
wrap ✳ Stones ✳ Old padlocks and chains

TIMING

When the moon is not in the sky

THE SPELL

✳ Put a small quantity of alcohol, gambling chips, betting slips, or drugs belonging to the offending person in the bubble wrap with a padlock and chain wrapped around it.

✳ Place the package in the box, add stones, secure it with more padlocks and chains, and say, [name offender], *there never can be enough, the deficit gets daily more, as down the drain you/our resources pour, this must stop, the habit drop, continue no more.*

✳ Bury the box in a deep hole weighed down with stones, saying, *Never more the light of day to see, addiction buried you must henceforward be.*

✳ Insist on rehabilitation.

Selling Your Debt

An onion ⋆ A sharp knife
⋆ A gold earring

TIMING

The night before a crescent moon

THE SPELL

* On the onion peel, scratch a minus sign and a dollar sign
  (or the sign of your local currency).

* Discard that layer and continue scratching the symbols, peeling and
  discarding until you have only the small white onion left.

* On that, scratch a plus and a dollar sign and cast the onion and the
  earring into the ocean, if possible, or into a river or lake. While casting
  the objects, say, *I sell this burden to the sea, return when you will as
  prosperity.*

If You Are Facing Bankruptcy or the Seizing Of Assets

YOU WILL NEED

A final demand, surrounded by a circle of six red candles ∗ A box of metal paper clips

TIMING

When the end seems close

THE SPELL

* Attach paper clips all around the edges of the demand, saying,
  On the strength of Mars do I call, when I am so low, there's nowhere to fall, so I reach upwards and aspire that growing light my cause inspires.

* Light the candles and clap your hands over each candle. Blow them out, relight them, blow them out, relight them, then leave and stamp three times while saying, *By the power of three, I will not defeated be, one last chance before I fall, on the cosmos, angels, human aid, and Mars I call, courage and power come alive, I can fight on, I will survive.*

* Make one last-ditch attempt at negotiation.

To Cure Shopaholic Tendencies

Ten beads on a bracelet or necklace ★ Ten items you
bought on impulse and never wore, placed in a basket

TIMING
Wednesday

THE SPELL

* Put on the bracelet/necklace and pick up each item in turn, saying,
  *Excess, more shall be replaced by less, no more shall be, this dire road to
  poverty, ten, nine, eight, seven, six, five, four, three, two, one, impulse
  buying is dead and gone, common sense has won.*

* Toss each item away.

* Now count each of your beads, saying, *Ten nine, eight, seven, six, five,
  four, three, two, one, impulse buying is dead and gone, common sense
  has won.*

* Sell unwanted or unworn items on eBay.

* Whenever you are tempted when shopping to buy in excess, stop and
  touch each bead on your bracelet/necklace and repeat all the spell words.

* Only then consider the purchase.

If Others' Unwillingness to Pay You is Bringing Down Your Business

YOU WILL NEED

A windup musical box with a figure on top ∗ Seven currency notes of any value

TIMING

Saturday for seven consecutive days

THE SPELL

∗ On day 1, wind up the musical box saying, *Round and round and round it goes, always the same song, my payment really is on the way, it surely won't be long, while I continue to scrimp and save and get deeper daily in debt, please pay me* [name a debtor] *within seven days, your obligations must instantly be met.*

∗ When the music stops, put the first currency note under the musical box and say, *Pay me, urgently, immediately or consequences you will see.*

∗ Continue each day, until all the notes are under the musical box. Then send final notices demanding payment in full within seven days.

To Succeed if You Have an Important Interview Concerning Consolidation or a Rescue Package

YOU WILL NEED

Silver foil ✶ A deep bowl of salt ✶ A turquoise or lapis lazuli crystal, preferably on a chain ✶ A sealed cloth bag ✶ Three sandalwood incense cones on a flat dish

TIMING

A few days before the interview

THE SPELL

* Seal the crystal in the bag and immerse the bag in the salt for twenty-four hours.

* Then take it out and light the incense, passing the crystal through the smoke of all three incense cones three times while saying, *Triple power, triple authority, convincing and confident will I be, the powers that be will listen to me, and so my consolidation/loan shall I see.*

* When the incense is cooled, mix the ash with some salt and put the mix in three twists of silver foil.

* Open and tip out the contents at three locations near the venue and wear the crystal.

A Credit Card Spell to Reduce Plastic Borrowing

YOU WILL NEED

Your credit cards in a row, highest owing or highest interest
to the left, in descending order ∗ A small box with a
lid ∗ Five orange or sage incense cones on a dish

TIMING

Before shopping

THE SPELL

∗ Light the incense cones and collect your cards in a pile.

∗ Deal them to yourself quickly, like you're playing cards, and say, *Not
playing a good hand, not getting a good deal, these must go for I do know,
the interest is unreal.*

∗ Put one card in the box, continuing until all the cards are in the box.

∗ Close the lid with a bang, saying, *Shut away and you must stay, until your
interest I can pay.*

∗ Tip the cooled ash outdoors.

∗ Take the card with the lowest interest shopping and, bit by bit, plan to
reduce the others one at a time.

CHAPTER 16

Avoiding Costly Scams, Cons, Frauds, Computer Hacking, AND Too-Good-To-Be-True Offers IN Love AND Life

Telephone and internet scams have become increasingly common as technology continues to develop. So, too, have get-rich-quick schemes, fraudulent pension investments, and plots against those trying to figure out the best ways to use their retirement funds. Equally as frustrating, rogue builders and contractors can step in for an emergency and then extract large sums for very little work.

While it's important to take earthly precautions, spells offer a protective shield to make us a bit more resistant to fraudulent and scam-like attacks—whether the scammer works through dating sites or you fall under the control of an unscrupulous online clairvoyant who promised to remove a curse or the bad luck you've been experiencing.

Worst of all is when a relative or trusted caregiver is taking advantage of an elderly or sick patient and no one believes you. Spells can open the way to reveal the truth. And, while we shouldn't interfere in the free will of others, we can help from the sidelines if we see them being taken advantage of, just as we would if they were in physical danger. In such cases, add to the spell, "if it is right to be." This way, you won't be interfering with the natural order of things.

To Prevent a False Clairvoyant Conning You into Buying Cheap, Useless Amulets from Them Supposedly to Ward Off Curses

One of the amulets (throw away the rest) ★ A silver-colored letter opener ★ An old red scarf ★ Cinnamon powder and dried cloves, placed in a bowl behind the amulet ★ Four white candles in a square around everything

TIMING

After receiving a demand

THE SPELL

* Light the four candles clockwise.

* Stir the herbs in the bowl with the knife nine times counterclockwise, then tap the knife point into the center of the amulet, saying, *All power against me begone, your* [name clairvoyant] *false claims are lost and done.*

* Place the amulet in the center of the cloth.

* Sprinkle herbs on top of the amulet, tie the scarf with three knots, and repeat the words.

* Leave the candles burning.

* In the morning, toss the knotted scarf into an outdoor garbage bin.

If a Cult or Unscrupulous Coven Online or Offline is Pressuring You for Regular Payments with Underlying Threats if You Don't

YOU WILL NEED

Children's dark blue modeling clay
★ A small piece of white modeling clay
★ Red thread on a ball ★ Scissors

TIMING

After unwelcome communication

THE SPELL

* Make a small, featureless figure in white clay to represent yourself. Then make blue clay figures to represent each key threatening person. Arrange the blue figures so that they are holding hands around the white clay figure.

* Tangle thread around the figures and loosely around your inactive hand.

* Cut those loops, saying, *You say you bind me magically, but I know it's down to money, you frighten and intimidate, and for payment will not wait.*

* Continue to cut all the tangles free, remove your figure, and roll the blue clay back into a ball.

* Bury the clay ball with a few coins in a hole saying, *The last payment now is sent.*

If You Strongly Suspect a Close Relative, Friend, or Professional Carer is Stealing from a Vulnerable Relative

YOU WILL NEED

A small, brown play clay figure with extra-long arms ∗ Blue thread ∗ A plastic tube of seeds

TIMING

Before a visit

THE SPELL

∗ Secure the thief's symbolic arms with thread, saying, *Stealing from a friend/relative/client I draw the line, taking advantage of the vulnerable is wicked and unkind, I bind you from further thieving and trickery, only when you desist will I set you free.*

∗ Squeeze the tied figure into the plastic tube so it is buried in the seeds, saying, *I separate you from your source of greed, you profit yourself and leave* [name victim] *in dire need.*

∗ Hang the tube on a tree or bush outside the victim's home saying, *Count the seeds till your wrong you see, only then shall you be free.*

To Escape from a Charismatic Guru Who is Bleeding You Dry with Expensive Treatments, Yet Insists Your Health Depends on Them

YOU WILL NEED

A white candle behind a dark purple strong thread

TIMING

Before meeting your guru

THE SPELL

* Light the candle, saying, *Light bright, take from my sight, this charismatic intensity, that makes me part unwisely with my money. When with you, I fall under your spell, as your latest products to me you sell.*

* Extinguish the candle.

* Loosely bind your hands with the cord, saying, *I no longer am bound within your thrall, I deny your power my mind to call.*

* Slip off the cord and loop it over an outdoor tree or bush.

* Relight the candle before any meeting, saying, *Be gone from my sight, I am guarded by light, your true self is ringed with dollar signs, spend the resources of others if they allow, but no longer mine.*

If One Too Many Valuables or Money Goes Missing After a Certain Person Visits Your Home

YOU WILL NEED

A string of garlic bulbs * A green candle * A dish of salt * The name of the person written backwards in red ink on blue paper

TIMING

The day of the visit

THE SPELL

* Block out each of the letters, starting at the end. Then rub each of the garlic bulbs in turn over the paper, from top to bottom and left to right, while saying, *Unwritten is your name, your deeds are just the same, barred you are, restrained and bound, no more can your thieving be found, all is protected, you are ejected.*

* Hang the garlic bulbs in the kitchen and make sure to keep the visitor there. Say the words in your mind as you enter behind the visitor.

To Prevent Yourself from Falling
for Internet Frauds or Scams

YOU WILL NEED

Three miniature toy goblins or imps, set along the front
of your computer, left to right * Three imp images in a
row on the internet, left to right, on another screen
* A drawstring bag

TIMING

After major new internet scams

THE SPELL

* Shut the first imp in your clasped hands while looking at the imp screen, saying, *Three nasty imps, sitting in a row, looking oh so innocent but havoc create we know, wiping out programs, emptying bank accounts, you are a total menace, off you must go.*

* Drop it into the bag and close it tight.

* Repeat the words and remove the left-most imp from the screen.

* Do the same for the second imp, changing the words to, "*Two nasty imps*" and finally, "*One nasty imp.*"

* Take the fastened bag and keep it with any broken or obsolete computer equipment you no longer use.

If Fraud is Happening at Work with Senior Management for Which You Could Be Blamed Even Though You're Innocent

YOU WILL NEED

Powdered lemongrass in a container ✷ A plate
✷ A small red bag ✷ A small, sharp implement
belonging to the workplace

TIMING

Wednesday before anyone arrives

THE SPELL

✷ Sprinkle lemongrass over the plate, saying, *Protect me from these human snakes, that they will make their own mistakes, and though they will seek me to blame, justice shall reveal their guilty names.*

✷ Write their names in the lemongrass with the sharp implement (it does not matter if it is not very clear), then shake the plate so the names are hidden, saying, *Hiding for now, but truth will out, and your uncovered dishonesty, will reflect badly on you not me.*

✷ Keep a little of the mix in the bag in your workspace. Wash the rest away in the workplace's bathroom.

If You, a Relative, or Vulnerable Friend Are in the Grips of a Rogue Builder, Electrician, or Plumber

YOU WILL NEED

A small item, even a nail, from the botched building work * A business card or demand for cash from the rogue builders, set in front of an unlit, half-burned grey candle * A new blue candle

TIMING

When a new demand is received

THE SPELL

* Light the half-burned candle, extinguish it immediately, and say, *Half a job is not better than none, the stress you've caused, the damage you've done, this must stop you must be gone.*

* Rip up the card and the copy of the demand, shred or cut up the candle, and dispose of them.

* Light the new candle, saying, *A fresh start, of which you are not part, banished you are, so go away far.*

* Seek instant legal redress.

For Recovery After Fraud Has Stripped You of Your Assets and Pension Rights

YOU WILL NEED

A tray containing sand ⋆ A deep pot filled with soil ⋆ Green plants ⋆ Five moss or tree agate crystals or jade and a clear quartz

TIMING

The end of a month

THE SPELL

* Flatten the sand, tip it out on barren land, and say, *Barren and futile, though we fight on, the old assets may forever be gone.*

* Put the plants in the soil and say, *Yet shall we start again, our efforts won't be in vain, new life, new ingenuity, a different future than planned before, we can and will regrow our finances faster more and more.*

* In the plant pot, put an agate or jade in each corner ~~and~~ the center.

* Keep the quartz in water and store this in

* Pour the water weekly on the plants to he

To Recover After the IRS or a Credit Card Company Has Unfairly Bankrupted You and Taken Your House

YOU WILL NEED

A tall, empty glass jar with a lid ✳ Sparkling glass nuggets or even glitter ✳ Different-colored sands in separate jars ✳ A small scoop

TIMING

The beginning of the month

THE SPELL

✳ Hold the jar, saying, *We'll leave you with nothing, they said, and they did, they thought that would be the end, our future seemed dead, but rise shall we through the pain, rebuild, regrow and we shall thrive again.*

✳ Put a layer of colored sand in the jar, adding some sparkly glass nuggets, and repeat the words.

✳ Put a lid on the jar and display it where natural light will shine on it.

✳ Each time you make a small step, add another layer of sparkle and colored sand, until the jar is full and your finances are restored.

To Prevent Virus Attacks or Hackers Shutting Down Your Website or Business

The main computer or tablet you work on ✱ Six green and black malachite crystals that protect all technology from harm ✱ Six tree incense cones on a dish

TIMING

Wednesday

THE SPELL

✱ Before switching on the machine, light the incense cones and, while holding the six malachite crystals in your writing hand, stand in the breeze of a nearby window and allow the smoke to waft over the malachite crystals in your other hand. While doing this, say, *Protection be against all attacks against my machine/s, turn back your viruses, thwart your hacking, let any threats disappear in smoke as if they never have been.*

✱ Take the incense outdoors to burn away. Set the malachite crystals on each corner of the machine. Put one in the center along the front, and one in the center along the back.

265

When You Connect with an Internet Twin Soul Who Asks for Financial Help to Be with You

YOU WILL NEED

A photo of you and a photo of your internet twin soul printed out on a single sheet ⋆ A small, lidded metal container of coins

TIMING

Before going online

THE SPELL

* Touch each picture in turn, saying, *You make me happy, all the right things you say to me, my heart tells me you are the prince/princess of my dreams, but is all as it seems?*

* Rattle the coin tin over the printout, saying, *Is it me or is it my money, that makes you talk your words of honey? Show yourself in your true light, then I'll know if you are Mr/Ms Right.*

* Burn the images, saying, *Travel over land and sea, find a way to come to me, if you will our life we'll share, otherwise you're just not there.*

* You soon will know.

If a Lonely Friend or Relative Plans to Move Overseas to Be with a Gorgeous Internet Lover and Invest Savings in Their Business

YOU WILL NEED

A packet of small colored novelty wedding favors, such as hearts or horseshoes * Fresh flower petals

TIMING

Before they sign anything

THE SPELL

* Scatter circles of favors indoors, saying, *Wishes can and do come true, love can last forever, but wait, be sure, that without investment love will still endure.*

* Scatter the petals outdoors, saying, *Let caution be your Good Fairy, if this is right, when midnight strikes, you can have security, but if your prince just disappears, you will still have your money to dry your tears.*

* Collect the favors and put them away in a box. Persuade the lovesick friend or relative to wait for at least a month and take financial advice. Arrange a safe meeting on home territory before releasing any funds.

If You Know a Partner or Relative is Conning You Financially, but You Don't Seem Able to Say No

YOU WILL NEED

A mirror in which you can see your head and shoulders ⋆ Six small, white battery tealights or candles, placed along the base of the mirror ⋆ Two large, dark-colored feathers, one in each hand

TIMING

In total darkness (apart from the candles)

THE SPELL

* Switch on the candles. In the dim light, cross the feathers over and around your head and shoulders (high and low and in spirals). Gaze into the mirror and say, *As the darkness of the mirror does not penetrate, so may your guilt and intense emotions, your binding words of obligation, be reflected back from me that I will no longer be drained by you through my kindness, financially. I extinguish this light.*

* Turn off the candles.

* Set the feathers upright in soil or pots on either side of the front door before the visit.

If You Are Pressured to Invest in Property in a Country with Few Safeguards But Potential High Profit

YOU WILL NEED

A set of three dice
* Three more dice shut in a box

TIMING

Before you finally decide

THE SPELL

* Shake the three dice in your hands three times. Roll them on the table and say, *Speculate, high stakes, risks to take, to play my Ace, intuition guide me.*

* Add a fourth dice to your throws, saying, *Could win spectacularly or lose dramatically, intuition guide me.*

* Add the fifth dice, letting them scatter, saying, *Unknowns, uncertainties, I must embrace, could end up a millionaire or with egg over my face, intuition guide me.*

* Add the final dice, saying, *Much variability, I need to have more certainty, intuition guide me.*

* Put your facts and figures together. Before finally deciding, repeat the spell and trust your intuition.

CHAPTER 17

Prosperity Through Markets, Fairs, Online Sales, Internet Stores, Exhibitions, AND Workshops

In the modern world, many people make money through their creations and talents by selling via the internet on various online stores (this includes book publishing).

Markets, fairs, and exhibitions can also provide a fruitful source of income from the sales of our personally created goods and services. With the internet, we can just as easily sell our products to the farthest corners of the world as we would to locals in our town. The internet can also enable us to teach and run online courses around the world, supplementing written, audio, and video material with live teaching. It can also be especially receptive to spells, as magick and cyberspace use similar energies.

If you are offering services online via skype, phone calls, or online group services, a magical boost can make you stand out positively and protect you from fraudulent clients. And, in an area where many have similar interests, it can be hard to be accepted as a newcomer, so magical protection can assist you in establishing yourself. Above all, it can help you realize your full marketing potential.

To Obtain a Stall in a Prime Location at a Market or Fair

YOU WILL NEED

A printed plan of the venue, showing stand positions * Four sparkling citrine crystals and a small sagebrush stick, placed in a pot

TIMING

Before booking your stand

THE SPELL

* Set a citrine in each corner of your chosen space.

* Light the smudge and spiral the smoke around the chosen site on the plan, saying, *Make this a place of high visibility that all will see, may all notice my stall favorably and time and again return to me.*

* Draw a smoke knot over each citrine and say, *Wind and bind the interest tight, that from the time I do begin, I will know this site is right.*

* Leave the smudge outside to burn away.

* Set your citrine in the four corners of your actual site and, if possible, smudge the physical area before beginning the event.

If You Are a Newcomer at a Market or Fair and the Other Stallholders Are Hostile and Cliquey

An obsidian arrow pointing outwards, paired with a pointed clear quartz, pointing inwards, placed at each corner of the stall

TIMING

As you set up

THE SPELL

* Using the index finger of your active hand, touch each obsidian and crystal point in turn, saying, *This marks my sanctuary, where all who enter will positive be, animosity and hostility I do return, threefold till good manners unfriendly folk do learn, come in peace or not at all, your barbs and arrows against my walls do fall.*

* Once you have set up your stall, circle yourself and the back-left crystal pair clockwise with clear quartz (in your active hand) and counterclockwise with obsidian (in your other hand). Then walk all around the stall waving the crystals and repeating the words.

To Launch Your Products and Services for the First Time in the Public Domain

YOU WILL NEED

Your products and publicity material together in one place * Twelve battery candles, organized in a row behind them, one for each month of the year

TIMING

Before setting out

THE SPELL

* Light each candle in turn, left to right, and, starting with the current month, name a candle for each month of the year, until you have lit and named all twelve candles.

* When all twelve candles are alight, pass both your hands flat (and palms down) over the products and publicity materials while saying, *May my creations be filled with light, every day, month, and year, that all may view them with delight, as success moves ever near.*

* Switch off the candles.

* At the venue, light the candles around your space, repeating the spell when you have set up your display.

If You Are Offering Psychic or Healing Therapies in a Noisy, Competitive Environment

YOU WILL NEED

A clear space before setting up

TIMING

Before anyone arrives

BANISHING

THE SPELL

* On the floor, walk to cover most of the area with the invisible shape of a protective banishing pentagram in visualized blue light.

* As you do so, say, *May only goodness and light here shine bright, let there be an enclosed space of peace, undisturbed healing without cease. So, I create this magical land, extending as far as I direct my hand.*

* Stand in the center of the invisible pentagram and extend your outstretched active hand at 45 degrees (fingers together).

* Turn around clockwise while visualizing a circle of blue light enclosing your space. Picture a doorway of white light for your clients to enter through.

* After the show, draw back the light through your fingers while rewalking the banishing pentagram.

If You Are Selling Plants, Herbs, or Healing Remedies You Have Grown or Created in a Market or Garden Center

YOU WILL NEED

A crystal pendulum, clear quartz, or amethyst * Trays of plants and herbs or healing remedies * Water left in natural light the previous day from dawn to noon

TIMING

Before packing

THE SPELL

* Hold the pendulum over each of your flat upturned palms in turn.

* Spiral the pendulum an inch slowly above each plant while saying the following words continuously, *Fill with the power of healing, infuse with the strength of greening, that what I sell, will make all well, my business thrive and come alive.*

* Sprinkle each plant with sun water before transporting.

* On arrival, spiral the pendulum clockwise around the tray/s, saying, *So shall my business grow, attracting wealth, not just as money but healing, harmony and health.*

For Selling Your Services and Creations at a More Prestigious Event or Major Outlet

YOU WILL NEED

An advertisement of the event or outlet
where you want to exhibit

TIMING

Full moon day at noon

THE SPELL

* Put your non-writing hand on your navel, which is the seat of your inner moonpower and desire.

* Place your other hand in the center of your upper stomach (your solar plexus). Your inner sunpower links you directly to the sun.

* Now extend both hands horizontally, palms down, fingers tucked in so only the index fingers are extending, and press hard into the advertisement, saying, *Filled be with my inner moon and golden inner sun, that easily and swiftly for me a place here is won.*

* Repeat both parts and say the words nine times in total.

* Then call the agent directly or apply online.

If You Want to Publish Electronically

A printout of the planned front cover
* Brightly colored marker pens or paints
* The front book cover on your computer screen

TIMING

Before uploading

THE SPELL

* Using the printout, begin to color in, as brightly as possible, your printed cover with paints or marker pens, saying, *Leaping from the screen, in all its brilliance this is seen, a number one, folks it will stun, a major sensation to light the nation and the world, my electronic publishing career shall unfold.*

* When you have finished, turn to the screen and, using your design program, apply similar colors to fill the front cover with brilliance while repeating the words above.

* Before uploading the book, return the cover to its normal shades, but say the words once more.

279

For Boosting Your Website Profile and Sales

Your website in editing mode on the screen
★ A printout of the home page ★ Adhesive foil stars,
moons, and lucky symbols in multiple colors ★ Scissors
★ A small electric fan ★ Rose or sandalwood
potpourri in a bowl

TIMING

Wednesday

THE SPELL

280

* Onscreen, cover your home page with stars, moons, and lucky symbols saying, *Throughout the world shimmer bright, that all will find me, all will see, and my reputation across cyberspace will guide the right clients increasingly, to find satisfaction in this place.*

* Stick stars all over the home page printout, repeating the words.

* Shred or cut the printout and, using the fan, scatter the pieces around the table and floor. Gather them and put them in the potpourri bowl near the computer.

* Leave just a few stars on your website.

For Successful Online Selling on eBay, Etsy, Gumtree, Facebook, or Any Other Online Portal

281

YOU WILL NEED

Your tablet or smartphone * A twig with leaves and, if possible, buds or blossoms, found, not broken off

TIMING

Crescent moon and the next three days

THE SPELL

* Visit each selling site you use or would like to use.

* Holding or resting your tablet/phone in the hand with which you do not write, gently pass the twig close to the screen, saying, *Thrive, come alive, travel through cyberspace, reach the places and people with whom I can make connection as though face-to-face.*

* When you have done this for each site, put the twig in water. Repeat the spell for the next three days.

* Set the twig in soil on a hill and let it blow free.

For Teaching, Counseling, and Mentoring Using Video Calling Programs and Social Media

YOU WILL NEED

Fish in a pond or aquarium you can feed
* Fish food * A small, silver bell

TIMING

Wednesdays

THE SPELL

* Ring the bell softly near the pond, saying, *I call you to hear me, wherever you may be, from far and near, I can help you fix your pain, assist you to laugh and smile again.*

* Put a little food on the surface of the water to interest the fish and repeat the words.

* As more fish come to be fed, scatter the food on the water, saying, *I will nurture all your needs, be a friend in times of sorrow, together through the airwaves, heart to soul, we will find a new tomorrow.*

* Ring the bell again.

* Repeat the spell regularly.

To Create a Successful Market Online and Face-to-Face for a Unique Product

Popcorn * A pan or popcorn maker * A large
bowl * An unusual flavor or spice

TIMING

The day before full moon

THE SPELL

* Cook the popcorn and toss it in the bowl afterwards nine times, saying, *Pop, pop. pop, hop and never stop, totally original, completely unique, not the same as the crowd for new markets I seek.*

* Add the spice to the popcorn and shake the bowl nine times again to mix it in. Say, *Roll, roll, roll, my future shall unfold, online and face-to-face, I shall take prime space in the marketplace.*

* Eat the popcorn.

283

To Start Your Own Online
Broadcasting Station or Program

YOU WILL NEED

A globe of the world on a stand

TIMING

The beginning of a month

THE SPELL

* Spin the globe, saying, *Once it was dials and wires, now I broadcast where I desire, I call you from East, South, North, and West, exciting features, fascinating guests, are you listening, waiting world? My broadcast is soon to be unfurled, it's different from the rest.*

* Spin the globe faster, saying, *Broadcasting to span the globe, so my prospects spin, capture the airwaves, new listeners daily win, news and topics, opinions galore, you listen once and then want more.*

* Spin the globe even faster, letting it come to rest, saying, *And so I start in modest ways, increasing tenfold every day, as my broadcasts are unfurled, they burst upon the waiting world.*

* Start as soon as possible.

If You Keep Getting Turned Down by a Particularly Lucrative Venue or Association

YOU WILL NEED

A flight of tall, wide steps

TIMING

The night before full moon night

THE SPELL

* Jump up two steps, then one step down. While doing this, say, *Two steps forward, one step back, it's not the talents I do lack, they never give me a chance, excuses, delays, maybe another day, they say, leading me a merry dance.*

* March up three steps and go back one, saying, *Getting nearer, won't accept no, persist, resist and closer to admission will I go.*

* March up four steps and don't go back till you reach the top, saying, *I simply refuse to be deterred, ever onward am I spurred, turn no to yes, ask more not less, and so I win, the hallowed precincts I've entered in.*

* Make another approach.

To Establish a Successful New Social Media Network or Dating Site

YOU WILL NEED

A tub of white rice * A small tub of sunflower seeds

TIMING

Early on the first day of the month

THE SPELL

* Shake the tub of rice while saying the following words continuously, *Facebook, Twitter, Instagram, these we all do know, dating sites galore, social media by the score, but there is a space for something new, a network that offers more.*

* Add the seeds to the rice and shake the container, saying, *Making something new is my aim, for all the rest seem much the same, lucrative they are, but I'll be the star, I'll start a new broadcasting game.*

* Scatter the mix far and wide in ever-widening circles outdoors, saying, *And so my social network profile will increase, not creating like for like, but finding the missing piece.*

* Launch your idea.

If You Are Working Two Jobs but Want to Concentrate on Selling Your Creations or Services

YOU WILL NEED

A path that splits in two, one overgrown, one well-trodden

TIMING

Early Sunday

THE SPELL

* Stand at the junction, one foot on either side, saying, *A foot on two very different paths, afraid to take the leap, and so I juggle, duck, and dive, and to neither road do keep.*

* Step on the untrodden path, saying, *I have my dream, now I must choose, risk all or fulfilment lose.*

* Continue to walk along the overgrown path, saying, *It will not be easy, torn two ways most every day, yet shall I stick to my choice, the future's mine to make, this path is here to take, in it I will rejoice.*

* Go back when you are ready. You may need to repeat the spell many times before you actually take the leap of faith.

CHAPTER 18

Prosperity Through Bargain Hunting, Antique Fairs, Auctions, Rummaging AND Prospecting, Renovations, AND Restorations

W hen we talk of treasure troves, we may think of pirates and buried chests filled with gold. But a number of people do make considerable profits by going to auctions and purchasing old items, from unwanted jewelry to valuable artifacts. Garage and car-trunk sales can also, especially in the early morning, offer hidden treasures. Increasingly, the buying, restoring, and selling of objects like furniture, tapestries, motorcycles, and cars is becoming a lucrative business.

Metal detectors haven't entirely replaced traditional dowsing, which involves using a forked hazel rod paired with a bent copper wire. The wire dips and vibrates when it has located something you have specified you wish to find beneath the ground. Similar activities include fossicking for minerals, prospecting for gold or opals, or buying small mining claims. Such activities are undergoing something of a revival, particularly in the US and Australia.

Archaeological digs can also reveal ancient treasures, and spectacular hoards have been discovered by individuals digging in fields (even in their own gardens). When foraging, the more you trust your intuition, the more likely you are to score. The spells in this chapter enhance those natural finding instincts that go back to the ancient hunter-gatherer tradition. They help draw you to the right place and bring what you seek into range.

To Find Treasure on a Formal or Informal Excavation or Archaeological Dig

YOU WILL NEED

A wide, flat tray of sand ✳ A map or plan of
the area you intend to dig that will fit flat into the tray
✳ A small, soft brush and pan ✳ A small cloth bag

TIMING

The day before the planned excavations

THE SPELL

✳ Press the map into the sand on the tray and scatter sand from the tray
to almost cover it, saying, *Deep beneath the sands of time, lies magick and
mystery, may buried treasure be revealed to me, from centuries of history.*

✳ Sweep off the sand into the pan and carefully tip a little into
the bag, saying, *Reveal your hidden secrets to me, that I may
make wondrous discovery.*

✳ Take the bag of sand and scatter it close to the dig area.

If You Want Regular Success on an Archaeological Dig or Using a Metal Detector for Finding Coins or Valuable Metals

YOU WILL NEED

Your excavating tools or metal detector

TIMING

Before a dig or excavation at the site or area where you will take your metal detector

THE SPELL

* Take a handful of earth from the site and say, *Treasure beneath the earth, to be given rebirth, though buried deep inside, again you shall be born, from ancient form, no longer shall you hide.*

* Follow your instincts on where and how deeply to dig or probe. While doing this, say the following words in your mind, *Show to me, what I need to see, to the surface undiscovered knowledge bring, reveal of value everything, not to disturb nor to harm, but leave the place undamaged and calm.*

If You Take Up Prospecting as a Serious Hobby with the Hope of Turning It into a Small Business

293

YOU WILL NEED

A small piece of whatever you are prospecting for

TIMING

The beginning of a month

THE SPELL

* Hold the metal/mineral and drop it into a small existing hole or crevice on a potentially fruitful site, saying, *Like for like, same to same, may I find this treasure as I speak its name* [name what you want to find].

* Mark the spot with a stick or distinctive stone.

* Walk in ever-widening circles around the area, repeating the words softly.

* Before beginning prospecting, return to the place you dropped your treasure and move both hands clockwise and horizontally over the spot, repeating the words.

To Dowse for Oil, Water, Gas, or Minerals as a Second Career

YOU WILL NEED

Either a single wooden, usually hazel, rod, holding
the short ends, one in each hand, that will dip down over the
subterranean target spot, or a pair of copper or brass or angle rods,
one in each hand, that will cross over the underground target

TIMING

Sunrise

WOODEN 'Y' ROD

THE SPELL

* Hold your chosen rod/s and say, *You are my hands,
  you are my eyes, reveal to me what below the land does lie,
  treasure brings pleasure and profitability to me.*

* Specify what you are looking for, for example a watercourse.

* Walk, totally relaxed, over the chosen area. Let yourself be
  guided by the subterranean lines. While doing this, repeat
  the words in your mind as a mantra. You will feel vibrations
  as you hit the subterranean seam or line, and your rod will
  dip or cross over the key places.

To Find a Valuable or Unusual Treasure to Sell or Renovate at a Sale Among What Looks Like Junk

YOU WILL NEED

A small mirror to fit hidden inside your active hand

TIMING

In sunlight/bright daylight

THE SPELL

* Before going to the place where you hope to find treasure, open your hand and flash the mirror so it catches the light of the sun/ daylight. While doing this, say, *Gleam bright, shine your light, that I shall be guided to where, I will find real treasure there, I follow you, to show me true.*

* Continue making light beam circles and saying the words, then pop the mirror in your pocket or purse, taking it to the sale.

* Hunt, picturing the light beams directing you to the right place. If desired, subtly hold the mirror in your non-writing hand.

To Find Unexpected Treasure at a
Dark Early Morning Antique Fair,
Garage Sale, or Car-Trunk Sale

YOU WILL NEED

A flashlight

TIMING

The night before the sale, after dark, outdoors

THE SPELL

* Stand in darknessand say, *I call on light to make all right, to reveal more, that tomorrow I may find treasure no one else saw.*

* Switch on the flashlight and turn in all directions on the spot in the darkness (clockwise and counterclockwise). While doing this, swirl the flashlight and say, *Light makes all right, attracting treasure within its beam, showing me more than I could dream.*

* Switch off the flashlight and go to bed. When you wake up, shine it again in the early morning darkness and repeat both sets of words.

* If it's still dark when you reach the sale, use the flashlight to examine the stalls. If it's getting light, picture the flashlight beam guiding you to the treasure.

To Get a Real Bargain at an Auction

YOU WILL NEED

A pointed, smoky quartz crystal

TIMING

While wandering around pre-auction

THE SPELL

* Choose the item or items you wish to bid for.

* Hide the smoky quartz point-outwards in your writing hand. Subtly pass it over or near the item/s while saying the following words in your mind, *I cast this cloak of invisibility, that through the mists other buyers may not see, for this* [name desired treasures] *is alone for me, hidden in the mists of obscurity.*

* When the bidding begins, hold the quartz hidden in the hand with which you do not write.

To Start a Successful Renovation or Restoration Business Through Uncovering the Right Materials at Sales and Auctions and Via the Internet

YOU WILL NEED

A small, tarnished item you know is of value
and belongs to the same kind of furniture
or an item you wish to restore

TIMING

Monday morning

THE SPELL

* Polish the item clockwise slowly and mesmerically while saying the following words over and over, *Shine your beauty, show your worth, lovely will you be, beautiful for all to see, a work of art and so I begin my restoration/renovation hopefully and end profitably.*

* Continue polishing while repeating the words.

* Keep the item and polish it each Monday morning as you develop your business. Never sell it or give it away.

To Find the Right Item at the Right Price

A picture of the desired item, the ideal price
written on the back in blue pen ✳ A green candle
✳ A pot of soil ✳ A small meat tenderizer

TIMING

The beginning of the month

THE SPELL

✳ Light the candle and blow into the flame three times while saying the
following words three times, *Light the way, to where* [Name] *waits, at the
right price, in the right place, guide me tomorrow or better still today.*

✳ Rip a corner off the picture, singe it in the candle, and drop it in the
soil. Continue ripping and burning until the whole paper is in the soil.

✳ Pound the paper in the soil until it disintegrates into ash, saying,
*I release the energy, nearer and nearer shall my bargain find me, at the
right price, swiftly and easily.*

✳ Keep the pot and the soil until you find the bargain (or it finds you).

To Sell an Item for a Good Price at an Auction

YOU WILL NEED

The item to be sold * Seven small, battery-operated
candles circling the item, or, if very large, a
picture of it * A feather duster

TIMING

Seven nights before the auction

THE SPELL

* On the first night, light all the candles clockwise. Pass your hands palms
  flat and down over the item or picture seven times while saying the
  following words seven times, *Seven days, seven ways, I release you willingly
  at a good price, that will be nice, and you will bring the new owner
  pleasure, just as you were once my treasure.*

* Dust gently over the item/picture, saying, *Breaking all connection, go now
  in your new direction.*

* Switch off the candles and repeat the spell for the next six nights.

To Break into the Antique Trade if Antiques Have Always Been Your Passion

YOU WILL NEED

A very old item, the most valuable you can
afford to buy ✳ Four musk or patchouli incense cones placed
on a dish in front of it ✳ A mirror placed behind the item

TIMING

Twilight

THE SPELL

* Light the incense so you can see the item reflected in the mirror through the smoke.

* Waft the smoke with your hand, saying, *One becomes two, in this venture new, old becomes my new trade, and so my fortune shall be made.*

* Continue wafting the smoke, saying, *Through the mists of obscurity, through the veil of time, buying, selling what I love, old and lovely, expertly and knowledgably, this new trade is mine.*

* Use the item as your first collectible. Sell it and buy more.

To Receive a Good Offer from a Specialist Dealer for a Family Treasure or Rare Books

A smooth twig with a pointed end ✳ The photo
you will send to the dealer ✳ A business
card from the dealer ✳ Blue thread

TIMING

Before visiting/sending the photo to the dealer

THE SPELL

* Put the photo under the business card.

* Tie them together with thread in three knots.

* Touch the knots with the pointed twig end in your active hand, saying,
Three by three [name of the dealer], *you are bound by me, to sell my treasure/books profitably. When you see this you will be impressed, your customers offer more not less.*

* Touch the knots with the index finger of your inactive hand, repeating the words.

* Touch the photo/card with the twig and your index finger. While doing this, say the words again.

* Leave the wand across the photo/card for 24 hours before contacting the agent.

To Get a Particular Bargain at a Major Sale if There is a Lot of Competition

YOU WILL NEED

A bowl and wooden spoon * Powdered nutmeg
* Frankincense essential oil * A large piece of silver foil

TIMING

The Wednesday before the sale or auction

THE SPELL

* Shake the nutmeg into the bowl, add in a drop or two of essential oil, and say, *Frankincense, I would empower, this magical nutmeg at this hour, let it good fortune to me show, that all competition may swiftly go, and I success in bidding know. Lady Luck on me shine, to make* [name desired item] *mine.*

* Mix the spices and oil while quickly repeating the words. Then divide the mix between three twists of foil.

* On the morning of the sale, place one twist on the appropriate page in the event's catalogue, scatter the contents of one outside the building, and wash the third one down a bathroom sink (or basin) at the site.

To Be Given Something You Want More Than Anything in the World

YOU WILL NEED

A large, open, fragrant white rose, the symbol of
secrecy ✳ Rose essential oil or white rose fragrance

TIMING

Crescent moon

THE SPELL

* Whisper into the rose what you most want. Then add, *Rose, this is my
  secret, what most I do desire, I wished on stars, didn't get very far, yet I
  believe, if I don't say, my wish will come true one day.*

* Put the fragrance on your inner wrist (a pulse point for your heart) and
  say, *I wish, I wish with all my heart, that the cosmos will soon impart this
  and bring to my life unimaginable bliss.*

* Keep the rose in water until it fades, then mix the dried petals with rose
  potpourri. Add in some rose oil or the white rose perfume to fragrance
  it. Refragrance it regularly.

To Barter Down the Price of Anything from a House, a Car, or Technological Goods Using the Fehu Viking Rune

YOU WILL NEED

A red marker pen * A sticky label

TIMING

Before you begin bartering

THE SPELL

* Draw the Fehu symbol, the value for money rune, on the sticky label, saying, *By the power of Fehu* ("fayoo"), *make the price right, reasonable, and realistic, and well within my sights.*

* Attach the label to the pen so the symbol is outwards, saying, *May the vendor be open to bartering, open-minded in everything, that we may swiftly an agreement bring.*

* Use the pen to write your highest offer and your ideal price on a photo of the item. Draw the rune in the air over your computer or phone before beginning serious negotiations.

CHAPTER 19

Enjoying A Rich Life: Alternative Prosperity Through A Fulfilling Lifestyle AND Charitable Acts

Society is orientated towards what you earn and what you achieve rather than who you are. It is easy to develop a lavish lifestyle that can trap you in an ongoing cycle of monetary gains and losses. If you don't have sufficient money and are on a constant quest for prosperity, materialistic assets, and providing for the family, then it can, in time, cause serious emotional burnout.

There are people who decide to step away from the rat race of life, to downsize, or to start an eco-business. Others decide to try their hand at following a dream, caring for animals, traveling around the world while homeschooling their children, or doing volunteer work to replace a previously unfulfilling, though lucrative, career.

Even if you don't quit your job immediately and decide to travel the world, the spells in this chapter are a reminder that life is for living now. Sometimes it benefits us to pursue dreams for the sake of clarity rather than external profit.

To Step Off the Frantic 24/7 World Dash and Live in a More Authentic Way That Will Bring Happiness

YOU WILL NEED

A globe on a stand

TIMING

When life loses its point

THE SPELL

* Spin the globe very fast so it almost tips, saying, *Stop the world, it spins too fast, making money that does not last, this is not the life I signed up for, happiness where did you go?*

* Spin it slower, saying, *Slow the world, give me space to breathe, time to pursue happiness, the treadmill to leave.*

* Slow it even slower, saying, *Slowing and showing, life possibilities, not 24/7, but a far better way to be.*

* Stop the globe and hold it, saying, *Not about the world, as around me it whirls, but all about me and tranquillity.*

* Make a plan to take some time away.

To Downsize Your Home and Move to the Coast or Mountains, Start a Hobby Farm, or Pursue Your Ideal Way of Living

YOU WILL NEED

Ice cubes * A saucepan * A spoon

TIMING

Noon

THE SPELL

* Put the ice cubes in the saucepan, add a little warm water, and say,
  The obstacles to happiness, are fears in my mind, leaving the security blanket of stress and the old world behind.

* Put the saucepan over a low heat, stirring it and say, *Let what is no longer needed go gently, following the dream that truly soon can be.*

* When the ice cubes are melted continue until steam starts to rise, saying, *From the old comes the new, from immovability new life shall break through, downsize and then rise* [name dream], *so all will see the better world can be.*

* Before all the water has gone, remove the saucepan from the low heat and pour it out.

To Quit the Rat Race and Take Yourself/Your Family to Explore Life on the Road or on the Ocean

YOU WILL NEED

A picture of your ideal boat or traveling vehicle * A stopwatch or digital timer

TIMING

The end of a month

THE SPELL

* Place the stopwatch on top of the picture. Set it for three minutes.

* While the stopwatch or timer is running, say the following words quickly and continuously, *Stop the clock, get off the wheel, adventure calls, the world I feel, beckoning, risk everything to gain all, I shall thrive and will not fall.*

* Set the stopwatch/timer for two minutes and repeat the spell. Do the same again for one minute.

* Hold the stopwatch/timer, saying, *The time gets nearer, for my big venture, take the first step and start the adventure.*

* Keep the stopwatch/timer and picture together and take the first steps. Repeat the spell whenever you hit a hitch.

To Quit the Pressures of Paid Work to Raise a Family or Focus on Creating a Beautiful Home and Garden

YOU WILL NEED

A small piece of real gold, such as an earring
* A small piece of iron pyrite, sometimes called fool's gold * A small gold bag * Gold thread
* A gold-colored letter opener

TIMING

Sunday

THE SPELL

* Put the pyrite in the bag, tie some thread around it, and say, *Tied with should and ought and must, the precious hours crumble to dust, the years flow away, life does not stay, we must live now for today.*

* Cut the threads, saying, *Set free to value the precious days, the golden moments that will not return again this way.*

* Set the real gold on top of the bag where light will shine on it and, while outdoors, cast the pyrite as far as you can.

To Work from Home in Order to Become More Self-Sufficient

The place where you will work from home * Two blue wax candles, placed in the center of the work room on a tray or broad holder * Twelve coins set around the candle * A new broom

TIMING

Monday morning

THE SPELL

* Light the candle and, as the wax begins to form a pool, drop the coins in it and say, *Let the riches of happiness come to me, even if modest the profits be, to have my own contented workplace sanctuary.*

* Sweep from the furthest corner of the room out of the door, saying, *Sweep away all misfortune and keep away stress, let this be a place of happiness.*

* Leave the broom, bristles up, outdoors outside the home front door.

* Cut out the wax circle of coins and keep it as your talisman in your new workspace.

To Homeschool Your Children as You Travel and Give Them Rich Life Experiences

YOU WILL NEED

A kite or helium balloon * Luggage labels,
brightly colored pens, and string

TIMING

Before you travel

THE SPELL

* Write on the luggage labels (get the kids to help if you wish) the places you would like to visit and things you would like to discover together and say, *The world is our school wherever we may be, a new classroom every day we'll see, viewing life in myriad ways, discovering new things, learning takes wings.*

* Attach the labels to the tail of the kite/balloon and release it.

* Make sure you fly a kite or balloon together early in your journeying.

To Find the Right Work in the Volunteer Sector with Friendly Coworkers if You Are Meeting Resistance

YOU WILL NEED

A special pen you will use on applications for volunteering ✳ A small piece of white paper

TIMING

Waxing moon

THE SPELL

* With the pen, cover a small piece of white paper in the name of your chosen charity and the words MAY I BE WELCOME.

* Fold it as small as possible and tap on it with the pen ten times, saying, *Open the doors, that I may give more, to those who lack, let not my fears or the feeling of being unwelcome hold me back.*

* Every morning, or just before an interview, if you feel unwelcome at the charity premises, subtly tap the door with the pen before entering and repeat the words.

* Put the paper in a wallet or purse and take it with you.

To Persuade Your Workaholic Partner to Slow Down

Two battery-operated or windup toy
trains placed side by side * String

TIMING

Waning moon

THE SPELL

* Set the trains side by side and set them in motion. While they're running, say, *Two trains on parallel tracks, no time to say more than "talk when I get back."*

* Put the trains on diverging tracks, saying, *You are making lots of money, for a future we don't share, working hard is your way of caring, but you're never there.*

* Stop the trains. Attach one to the other with string and say, *Stop, we're heading for a crash, all the gold in the world, is no good if the relationship's smashed.*

* Leave the two trains attached and motionless while saying, *Frantic days now are through, we shall share happiness, me and you.*

* Give the trains to a child.

If You Are Successful in a High-Powered Career but Your Heart is Not In It

YOU WILL NEED

Four gold-colored charms or medallions with
hooks * A gold-colored chain

TIMING

Any transition time, such as the end of a month

THE SPELL

* Thread the medallions/charms one at a time on the chain and place the chain around your neck. For each medallion/charm, say the following words, *Accolades and praises, promotion, promises of raises, but oh how heavy around my neck, is the glory worth it, is it heck?*

* Take off one medallion/charm while repeating the words and actions. Do this for each medallion/charm, until the chain is empty.

* Hold the chain in your cupped hands and say, *I no longer need even the weight of the chain, I am free and shall henceforward be my own true self again.*

* Make plans to quit the rat race as soon as feasible.

To Move Overseas to a Very Different Lifestyle at Any Age or Stage in Life

YOU WILL NEED

A pair of old, worn-out work shoes ⋆ A pair
of new beach shoes, deck shoes, or snow boots;
whatever is suitable for your desired location

TIMING

Full moon

THE SPELL

* Put on your old work shoes, saying, *You do not do, you do not do, worn-out shoes, long you have traveled the path of duty, but now I seek the way of beauty.*

* Put aside the old shoes for recycling. Put on your new shoes and, even if it's raining out, run outdoors and dance while saying, *New shoes, new shoes, splendidly you do, carry my feet to my new destiny, where a whole new life waits for me.*

To Become a Foster Carer of Children

YOU WILL NEED

A pin board with advertisements placed by
organizations to which you are considering applying that
arrange the foster caring of children ＊ Gold ribbons
and stars, crystals with adhesive tape on the
back ＊ A row of green candles

TIMING

Friday

THE SPELL

* Decorate around the edges of the pin board with ribbons, gold stars,
  and crystals, saying, *Find your pathway to our/my door, the riches of love
  there will be, happiness and security.*

* Hang the board on the wall and light the candles in front of it, saying,
  Follow the light to the door, in our/my heart/s there is always room for more.

* Send in your application and fill the board with photos of children
  you've fostered over the years (if any).

To Find the Right Place and Resources to Set Up an Animal and/or Bird Sanctuary

YOU WILL NEED

Small ceramic animals and birds, as many as you wish, arranged in a visualized spiral formation outward towards the center, like the diagram below ✳ A musk or patchouli incense stick placed outside the spiral

TIMING

Friday

THE SPELL

✳ Light the incense stick and follow the spiral shape in smoke in the air three times. Make sure to go above the outside of the coil, into the center, and back again. While completing these actions, say, *St. Blaise, St. Francis, and St. Anthony, Saints three, guide all creatures in need to my/our sanctuary, grant resources to make real this possibility, and that will be true prosperity.*

✳ Leave the incense to burn. Light incense weekly around the spiral of animals, until you are guided to the right place or resources. While doing this, call on the three animal and bird saints for aid.

To Start an Eco-Venture and Become Self-Sustainable Within Six Months

YOU WILL NEED

Six rosemary plants ✶ Six jade crystals, one soaking in a jug of water 24 hours before the spell ✶ A long trough of soil

TIMING

Two or three days before full moon

THE SPELL

* Plant your rosemary in the trough. Sprinkle jade-infused water on it while saying, *Rosemary, rosemary, to my wishes incline, within six months let sustainability be mine, jade of immortality bring this venture to birth, making a difference to the earth.*

* Bury the jade in the soil.

* Each month for six months, add a rosemary plant to the trough two or three days before the full moon. Sprinkle the new plant with jade-infused water. Make sure the jade-infused water is fresh and that the new jade has remained inside it for 24 hours.

* Bury the new jade each month in the soil.

To Become a Carer for a Sick, Disabled, or Elderly Relative, Even if This Means Giving Up Your Career

YOU WILL NEED

A white candle ＊ Seven green ribbons

TIMING

Sunday evening

THE SPELL

＊ Light the candle, saying, *Light the way for me, that my new life path will be filled with peace and tranquillity.*

＊ Pass the first ribbon over the flame, then ribbon two. Tie a loose knot to join them and say, *I tie reserves of strength for each tomorrow, asking they will be days and nights of joy, not sorrow.*

＊ Continue until all seven ribbons are joined.

＊ Blow out the candle, saying, *I turn my back on the fast track, seeking riches in sharing and caring and knowing I shall nothing lack.*

＊ Hang the ribbon cord where you can touch each knot any time you need extra patience or understanding.

To Raise Money for a Person Who Needs Urgent Medical Attention or Aid

YOU WILL NEED

A bubble blower * Bubbles

TIMING

Early Sunday morning

THE SPELL

* Name the person for whom you are raising the money and the ultimate target.

* Blow your first bubble slowly, and as it rises say, *Raising targets, aiming high, calling in prosperity, that this urgent plea swiftly answered shall be.*

* Blow the second bubble equally slowly, saying, *The target [Name] shall be easily reached, limits very soon be breached, for this emergency the sky's the limit, and limitless the response shall be.*

* Blow bubbles faster. Between bubble blows, repeat the two sets of words alternately faster and faster, until all the words jumble together and the bubbles are gone.

* Then stand quietly and say, *This shall be, I call on the world's* [or specific place targeted] *generosity. Target attained, the right result gained.*

* Double your fundraising efforts.

CHAPTER 20

Spells FOR Prosperity Using Colors, Crystals, Metals, Herbs, AND Fragrances

For centuries, spells for prosperity, like other everyday spells, have been cast using natural substances. Many have developed natural magical associations, for example acorns from the oak tree for slow-growing but solid prosperity; the fiery basil herb for a powerful, fast infusion of money; the color green, associated with growth; and frankincense, considered a royal fragrance and one of the most precious and valuable substances. Casting spells with certain elements at specific times also maximizes the power of the spell.

Anything that grows, whether a young plant or a mineral in the ground formed over millions of years, is especially potent as a symbol of increase. Colors are both an instant and ongoing focus in money spells and, if worn or carried after the spell, continue to spread through the day the powers that they contain. Each color has specific associations with angels, deities, days of the week, fragrances, crystals, and flowers, and because colors have been used in spells for hundreds or even thousands of years, they have spontaneously accumulated great power from these linked substances.

A Five Deity Fast Yellow Money Ritual for Urgent and Instantly Needed Money

YOU WILL NEED

A yellow bouncy ball ★ Five yellow ribbons

TIMING

Wednesday at first light

THE SPELL

* Attach the ribbons to the wrist of your active hand.

* Start bouncing the ball either up and down or against a wall,
  saying, *Thoth, Hermes, Mercury, swift messengers three,
  let swift money come urgently to me.*

* Keep bouncing the ball, saying, *Hermod and Iris making five,
  winged harbingers of fortune, make my fortunes come alive.*

* Bounce faster and quickly chant both sets of words, one after
  the other, until you can't go any faster, then catch the ball and say,
  *You who whizz ceaselessly through the skies, make I ask, my finances rise,
  send me [name amount needed] urgently, by the power of yellow
  make this be.*

* Wear something yellow all day.

A Brown Ritual for Stabilizing an Insecure Financial Situation

YOU WILL NEED

A heap of soil from around a thriving plant, set in
a deep tray or trough ∗ Four heavy brown stones
found locally ∗ Four coins, brown colored
if possible ∗ A brown flower

THE SPELL

∗ Flatten the soil.

∗ Around the edges of the soil, place the stones and the coins, alternating
between each, until a square is formed. While doing this, say, *Security,
stability, give weight to the situation* [Name], *that all may settle, quiet, rest,
and my finances turn out after all for the best.*

∗ Now place the coins beneath the base of each stone while repeating
the words.

∗ Put the brown flower in the center.

∗ Keep your tray where it will not be disturbed. Push the flower down
in the soil when it dies and replace it with another one. Do this until
matters are stabilized.

A Green Ritual for a Successful New Investment Where Luck is Initially Required

YOU WILL NEED

A leafy green bamboo plant ∗ Six green ribbons
∗ Six small, shiny green baubles or gold bells

TIMING

Friday

THE SPELL

∗ Attach the baubles or bells to the ribbons and then join the ribbons together, leaving the two ends knotted but free.

∗ Now drape the joined ribbons around the bamboo and spin each bauble/bell in turn. For each one, say, *Lucky bamboo, with your greening power, at this hour, I call on you my investments to grow, that I will rapidly know, in the months and years following, that instant and lasting success you will bring.*

∗ Whenever you tend your bamboo, twirl each bauble, repeating the words six times.

An Orange Ritual for Abundance and Happiness Through a Major Financial Success for Which You Have Worked Hard

YOU WILL NEED

A small spade ★ An orange carnelian crystal
or an amber ★ A pot of marigolds or other
small, many-petalled orange flowers

TIMING

Sunday

THE SPELL

* Stamp heavily in damp soil and scoop up your footprint soil with the spade. Place the soil into the marigold pot around the marigold roots while saying, *I imprint my success, I seek nothing less, than to bring me happiness and pleasure through the fulfilment of this endeavor.*

* Hold the crystal, repeat the words, and push it into the center of the marigolds so that the flowers will grow around it.

A Gold and Silver Ritual for Getting the Necessary Funds Fast to Fulfill a Dream

YOU WILL NEED

As many small gold- and silver-colored items as you can find * A stopwatch * A gold- or silver-colored dish * A picture of the kind of situation, place, or structure you dream of, set in the dish

TIMING

Full moon day at noon

THE SPELL

* Set the stopwatch for three minutes.

* Pile as many of the gold and silver items as you can into the dish on top of the picture before the three minutes is up.

* When time is up, run your fingers through the items in the dish, saying, *Accumulate more, fill my coffers by the score, masses of silver and masses of gold, dreams do not wait forever to unfold.*

* Each week add something to the dish, until it is overflowing. Then take steps towards the dream.

A Nine Blue and Brown Goldstone
Charm Bag for Making Serious Money
Through Marketing Your Talents

YOU WILL NEED

Five blue and four brown goldstone
crystals ★ Nine dried bay leaves ★ A small
magnet or lodestone ★ A green purse or
bag ★ Sweet almond oil or cooking essence

TIMING

Sunday, waxing moon

THE SPELL

* Shake the nine goldstones, saying, *Fortune smile on me this day, may the right opportunities come this way, that like these stones I may shine, and success and fame soon be mine.*

* Add them to the bag, followed by the bay leaves.

* Add the magnet, saying, *Draw to me, what I need for success and prosperity.*

* Finally, add a single drop of almond oil or cooking essence to the bag/purse, close it, and say, *May all I need come my way.*

* Keep your bag hidden in the room where you initially apply for opportunities.

A Rutilated Quartz Ritual for Finding a Totally Unexpected Source of Income or Resources When Most Needed

YOU WILL NEED

A rutilated quartz (clear quartz with gold needles within)   *   A mirror   *   Six small, gold candles placed in a row along the base of the mirror

TIMING

Monday

THE SPELL

* In total darkness, light each candle in turn, left to right. As you do this, look in the mirror and say, *Burn a pathway filled with gold, that unexpected resources may swiftly unfold.*

* Starting with the candle on your immediate left, hold the rutilated quartz to each candle's light and the words.

* Stand behind the candles in the center of the mirror. Look at the rutilated quartz in the mirror and say, *Burn a pathway of ingenuity that I will see, that new source of gold and infinite resources will unfold.*

* Blow out the candles and sleep with the quartz under your pillow.

A Five Citrine Ritual to Stop Thieving and Bad Practices Against Your Business

YOU WILL NEED

Five sparkling yellow citrine, the merchant's crystal, which protects against human snakes

TIMING

Before your premises opens or before you start work in your home office

THE SPELL

* Walk the banishing protective pentagram on the floor of your workplace, whether this is several rooms or a single room. Ensure that the uppermost point of the pentagram is near the main or outer door.

* Now place, hidden if possible, the five citrine in the position of the five points, again walking the shape as you set them. While doing this, say the following words continuously, *Be protection for my business and guardian to me, against all thieving, malice, and hostility, drive away all human snakes, keep pure and safe for me this place.*

* Citrine doesn't need cleansing, but rewalk the pentagram weekly.

A Red and Green Garnet Ritual to Stop Family or an Ex-Partner from Draining Your Resources

YOU WILL NEED

An unpolished red garnet and a green garnet

* A red candle placed behind the red garnet and a green candle placed behind the green garnet

TIMING

Waning moon

THE SPELL

* Light the red candle, saying, *Mars, let me not be argued down, that in fulfilling others' demands, my finances drown.*

* Light the green candle, saying, *The power of Venus let me resist, the emotional twist of guilt and unreasonable expectation, matched and mingled with false obligation.*

* Blow out both candles together, then relight them. Shake the crystals together in front of the candles while saying, *A new regime, gone is the soft touch, ask away, you won't get much.*

* Toss the crystals in the air, catch them, and blow out the candles fast.

* Keep the crystals in your purse or wallet.

A Seven-Day Brass Ring Ritual for Turning Your Fortunes Around Fast

YOU WILL NEED

Seven brass curtain rings or brass discs from a DIY
store　*　A strong gold curtain cord　*　A yellow cloth

TIMING

Bright sunlight, or substitute an adjustable desk lamp

THE SPELL

* Polish the first ring, and as you do so, slowly and continuously whisper,
  *Brass restore all, let me not fall, draw to me money within seven days,
  and let it stay.*

* Hold the ring to sunlight or lamplight whilerepeating the words.

* Hang the first ring on the cordand say the words again.

* Each day repeat the spell.

* On day seven, repeat the spell, then arrange the rings at regular intervals
  along the cord loop. After that, knot the two ends of the cord.

* Hang the cord high inside the front door, where light will shine on it.

A Triple Brass Bell Ritual to Shake Up a Stagnant Business or to Invigorate Your Investments

YOU WILL NEED

Three small, ornamental brass bells set in a row
* Three gold candles, one behind each bell

TIMING

When the weather is stormy or windy

THE SPELL

* Near a closed window, light the smallest candle to the left.

* Blow into the flame, saying, *Swiftly stir the energy, get the action moving vigorously shaking and grooving.*

* Ring the first bell while repeating the words.

* Light the second candle, blow into the flame, ring the second bell, saying, *Ringing and singing, life is zinging, move the money, make it dance, success pour in, leave nothing to chance.*

* Repeat with the third candle and bell, saying, *Flying high, dividends booming, business is zooming.*

* Open the window and let the wind blow out the candles.

* Ring the three bells in turn each morning.

To Succeed in a Major Promotion or Big Salary Increase

YOU WILL NEED

Fresh olive, ivy, bay laurel, or palm leaves ★ Copper wire cut
and bent to fit as a circle on the top of your head ★ Gold or
red ribbon ★ Strong gold thread or twine and scissors

TIMING

The day before full moon

THE SPELL

* Begin weaving the leaves around the circle of copper wire to make
  a crown, securing the individual fronds with thread so they overlap.
  While doing this, say, *All shall think highly of me, recommending a higher
  position/increased salary immediately, so I shall the victor be, and great
  success see instantly.*

* Put on the crown and take a selfie on your smartphone or camera.

* Pin the photo on the wall and make sure it's surrounded by the victory
  wreath. Next morning, send your application or arrange your meeting.

A Twelve-Month Copper Ritual to Keep Financial Luck and Opportunities Flowing into Your Home Through the Year

YOU WILL NEED

A circle of 12 small copper nuggets or 12 thin copper rings * Twelve green candles surrounding the copper circle * A pot with a lid in the center

TIMING

The beginning of a month

THE SPELL

* Light the first candle, name the current month, and say, *Bring to me what I need, for this month and through the year, that opportunity and money will continuously appear.*

* Set the first nugget in the pot, return the lid, and repeat the words.

* Blow out the candle.

* On the first day of the second month, name the new month and light the first two candles.

* Repeat the spell exactly, this time adding the second nugget to the pot.

* Continue each month, lighting one more candle and adding nuggets to the pot.

* On month twelve, leave the candles to burn.

A Tin Ritual Dedicated to Jupiter for Long-Term Financial Prosperity and Stability

TIMING

Thursday

THE SPELL

* Light the candle, saying, *By the power of Jupiter, I build up my security, for ten years and ten years more, stability and lasting security by the score.*

* Put the discs/coins one by one into the box, naming the next ten years. Start from the current year, and name one succeeding year for each disc/coin.

* When all are in the box, add in the ribbon with ten knots, then close the box. While doing this, repeat the words.

* Keep your box with your financial records. If you wish, put a lucky jade Buddha on top of the box.

A Signature Fragrance Ritual for Starting Your Own Business

Your favorite fragrance ✳ **Your favorite potpourri** ✳ **A bowl of water**

TIMING

Friday

THE SPELL

* While holding your fragrance bottle between your hands, say, *Be filled with my essence, fragrance of power, define me and make me successful from this hour.*

* Put a few drops of fragrance in the potpourri.

* Scatter three circles of potpourri around the bottle and candle.

* Add a little fragrance to the water bowl and scatter three circles of waterdrops on top of the potpourri circles.

* Anoint the center of your brow, the base of your throat, and each inner wrist point with the fragrance, repeating the words.

* In the morning, place the infused potpourri in your premises.

* Anoint the door handles and window latches with the perfume water.

* Each morning anoint yourself with the fragrance and repeat the words.

A Three-Rose Ritual for Reviving Your Fortunes After a Setback

YOU WILL NEED

A slightly fading yellow rose ★ A blossoming
red rose ★ A pink rosebud

TIMING

Sunset, dawn, and noon

THE SPELL

* At sunset, take the yellow rose outdoors, face the sunset, and say,
  *What is done is gone, wrong can't be right, so I let go of regrets and look to
  tomorrow's light.*

* Leave the rose and don't look back.

* At dawn, take the pink rosebud outdoors.

* Stand facing the dawn and say, *The door to the future will open once more,
  new ideas, new places, the old replaces.*

* Put your rosebud in water in your workplace.

* With the red rose, face the brightest place in the sky at noon, saying,
  *I will succeed, my finances revive, my hopes and my future are alive
  and will thrive.*

* Tie your red rose around a tree or bush.

A Chamomile Ritual to Get a Lucky Break in Your Present Career or to Open the Door to a Well-Paid Fulfilling Position

YOU WILL NEED

Three chamomile teabags ★ A mug
★ A small flask ★ Hot water

TIMING

Two days before the full moon and full moon day

THE SPELL

* On day one, split the first teabag and scatter the contents outside your front door while saying, *Good fortune hear my call, good luck answer my plea, bring that break and the right paid job for me.*

* On day two, make a mug of chamomile tea and sip it slowly while saying,
  I absorb good luck to answer my plea, to bring that break and the right paid job for me.

* On day three, or when you next go to work, make a flask of chamomile tea.

* Sprinkle it outside your workplace early in the morning, repeating both sets of words.

CHAPTER 21

The Dream Ticket: Obtaining THE Financial Resources TO Fulfill Your Greatest Desires

W e all want to live the dream—a life without having to worry about money. So, unlike most of the spells in this book, this chapter is based on how to achieve the dream through winnings. Through the power of manifestation, and if you believe with all your might that you want something enough, you might actually get it. After working hard for many years with little reward, you may want that one big win to give your family the life they deserve.

Spells in this chapter focus on helping you via the cosmos, angels, and what can guide you toward having enough money to last a lifetime, so that you might be able to enjoy yourself in your retirement years. There are spells for those who want to marry a kind and rich person, spells for receiving an unexpected inheritance, and spells to facilitate owning your own home.

This chapter is for the gray or rainy days when life seems too mundane. When we dare to dream, and believe in it enough, miracles can happen. There's nothing to lose, yet everything to gain. All the spells here represent dreams that people have expressed to me over the years.

The Ultimate Lottery Win

YOU WILL NEED

Five old lottery tickets with which you won small amounts
or nothing at all ✳ A fireproof container with sand in
the bottom ✳ A red pen ✳ A lucky bamboo plant
with red cord attached ✳ Five gold-colored coins

TIMING

When you feel lucky

THE SPELL

✳ Write across the numbers on each of the tickets, I SHALL WIN THE
  BIG PRIZE, I RELEASE THE VICTORIOUS POWER TO THE SKIES, I CLAIM
  MY WINNING DESTINY, THE RIGHT LOTTERY NUMBERS SHALL ROLL
  NOW FOR ME.

✳ Burn the tickets and bury the ash with five gold-colored coins beneath
  the bamboo.

✳ Buy your ticket if it feels right or repeat the spell until it does.

If You Dream of a World Cruise

A picture of your chosen ocean liner or a
private yacht ∗ A globe of the world

The beginning of a month

∗ Set the picture beneath the stand of the globe, saying, *Around the world, spanning the globe, on my dream boat, as fabulous sights unfold.*

∗ Spin the globe slowly saying, *Exotic lands, await, sounds, history, mystery, and when it's late I return to my cocoon of luxury.*

∗ Spin your globe faster and faster, saying, *The whole world on offer to me, it seems so close that I can see, the lights of my ship reflected on the sea, as dreams become reality.*

∗ Hold the spinning globe and deliberately slow it until it is still.

∗ Collect pictures of ocean liners and exotic ports on a pin or vision board.

To Have Sufficient Funds to Travel Wherever and Whenever You Want in the World

A door or an archway to a garden or park where
there are wild birds ∗ A bag of birdseed

TIMING

Waxing moon

THE SPELL

∗ Walk through the door or archway, scatter the seeds on either side, and
say, *Free to roam where I wish over land and sea, through desert, plains, and
mountains high, the world will come to me.*

∗ Continue walking until you reach an intersection of paths or roads.
If there are no crossroads when you are almost out of birdseed, create a
three-way mini-intersection with sticks or stones, saying, *Free to go in all
directions, choose my path at life's intersections, I give out to the cosmos this
energy, to return as necessary resources to me.*

∗ Deposit the rest of the seeds there.

To Restore a Mansion, a Stately Home, or a Chateau to Its Former Glory and Live in It

Four small, unpolished crystals still in the rock or matrix
★ A tumblestone amethyst in the center ★ A sagebrush
mini smudge stick ★ Five gold-colored coins

TIMING

Friday

THE SPELL

* Arrange the crystals in the garden of your present home or in a tray of earth in a small square with the tumblestone in the center.

* Light the smudge and waft the smoke with your hand around and inside the square four times in all, saying, *So do I lay the modest foundations for my great dream, impossible though to others it may seem.*

* Cast the coins in the center, saying, *I cast my fortunes to the winds, knowing the resources will me find, and from such beginnings will grow my grand designs.*

* Leave the smudge to burn.

To Sail Around the World in Your Own Boat

YOU WILL NEED

Any boat, however small, even a kayak or small sailboat on the ocean, river, or local lake, as long as you can paddle it alone.

TIMING

Wednesday, waxing moon

THE SPELL

* Say, *The water is wide and I would sail far, to the ends of the world and back, following my star.*

* Go as far as you can and then turn for shore, saying, *Though now to shore I do return, distant places across the water I yearn, I shall be captain of my ship, master/mistress of my craft, one day, the dream comes nearer when I shall sail away.*

* Take every opportunity to be around boats or crewing or take navigation lessons.

To Inherit an Unexpected Fortune

A money box * Sufficient coins of any denomination
to fill it, plus a clear quartz crystal

TIMING

Thursday

THE SPELL

* Add the coins and crystal to the money box and shake it three times, saying, *Hidden money, I cannot yet see, I call into my life, to make me wealthy.*

* Open the box and tip the coins into a heap. Run your fingers through the coins and say, *Though I do not directly know you, yet I shall welcome your bounty, whoever you are, wherever you be, I thank you for the inheritance you will pass on to me.*

* Keep the coins in the money box and do not spend them or allow anyone else to use them.

To Get a Substantial Payout or Huge Bonus from Money You Lost or Had Written Off Ages Ago

Four musk incense cones in in a row on a
heatproof tray * A grey or black feather

TIMING

Saturday near the end of a month

THE SPELL

* Indoors, light each cone. As you walk in ever-widening circles carrying the tray, waft the smoke in every direction with the feather and say, *Lost in the mists of time, forgotten in obscurity, yet will you find your way back to me, substantial money when least seems likely to be.*

* Take the incense outdoors while saying the same words. Let it go out or burn through, and let the feather blow away.

353

To Marry a Lovely, Kind, Generous, and Very Rich Person

354

YOU WILL NEED:

A small box of luxury chocolates or
exotic fruit ★ Two gold candles

TIMING:

Any consecutive seven days

THE SPELL

* Every evening light the first candle and then the second from the first, saying, *Bring to me a husband/wife true, kind, and generous, wealthy too and I pledge to care for you.*

* Eat a chocolate or fruit slowly and say, *And I will love you for who you are, not for your money or what you give me, but oh a little luxury, would make my life immensely happy.*

* Blow out the candles together.

* On day 7 leave the candles to burn through.

* Repeat the spell for six more days and then share the rest of the chocolates.

An All-Purpose Hamied Angel of Major Miracles Ritual to Save Yourself from Almost Inevitable Financial Disaster

355

YOU WILL NEED:

Seven small white candles in a circle   *   Seven snow or milky quartz or white howlite, one outside each candle   *   A jug of milk in the center

TIMING:

Noon, full moon day

THE SPELL

* Light the candles clockwise, saying, *Hamied, make possible what I cannot right now attain, shine your dazzling light and turn all loss to gain.*

* Leave the candles to burn, then bury each in a row to form a subterranean pathway leading from your front door or as close to your home as possible.

* On top, make a parallel pathway of milk, tipping it from the jug in a line, saying, *Hamied, I offer riches to the earth, in return, grant I ask this miracle sees birth.*

For Your Investments to Revive After a Previous Loss or Setback

356

THE SPELL

* Light the half-burned purple candle and sprinkle salt in the flame, saying, *What seems dead may rise again, though I believed all hope in vain.*

* Light the grey candle and sprinkle salt into its flame. Say, *Though I accepted my loss and moved on, suddenly I believe some good may come.*

* Light the white candle, sprinkle salt into its flame, and say, *Revive, come alive, when you will, I am not holding my breath, but magically I send this power that you may suddenly and bountifully thrive.*

That You Will Have Sufficient Resources for a Really Good Retirement in Spite of Gloomy Forecasts and Pension Losses

YOU WILL NEED

A pathway between trees leading out into an open space * Two red ribbons

TIMING

A sunlit day

THE SPELL

* Begin walking under the trees, saying, *I walk the path into future sunlight, despite gloomy forecasts, all shall be right.*

* When you reach the open space, turn around between the last two trees on the path and, while facing the path through the trees, say, *The way may sometimes be dark, choices may seem hard and stark.*

* Turn to face the open space, saying, *But I know resources will come, new sources of revenue and unexpected income.*

* Hang a ribbon on each of the trees, saying, *All shall be well, that I can tell and then go home another way.*

That You Can Afford Private Cosmetic or Restorative Surgery to Correct a Problem That Has Always Bothered You

YOU WILL NEED

A featureless outline drawn on white paper, one side in grey, the other in green ★ Scissors ★ Bright coloring pens in rainbow colors

TIMING

Any seasonal change point

THE SPELL

* Cover the grey outlined figure with dollar signs or your local currency symbol, saying, *People say it is all right, but I know it's not, it bothers me day and night, if I could pay for the remedy, life would then perfect be.*

* Turn the paper over, color the green outlined figure in rainbow shades, and say, *Confident shall I be, after the remedy* [Name] *able to function brilliantly, all I ask is the resources, from whatever place or good sources.*

* Cut out the figure and hang the rainbow side where it will catch the first light of day.

For a Permanent Home in a Safe Location for You and Your Family if You Are in Temporary Accommodations

A picture of the home you want ✳ Small worry dolls
or toy dolls for each family member ✳ A green
scarf or cloth ✳ Green thread ✳ Scissors

TIMING

Saturday

THE SPELL

✳ Wrap the figures on top of the picture in the scarf.

✳ Bind the scarf tightly with thread in nine knots and say, *I ask for my family, that there will be, a home where we can live safely, not unreasonable, you angels and guides please bring us lasting security.*

✳ Cut the knots and release the figures, repeating the words.

✳ Using the thread, attach the dolls to a bush or indoor plant and say, *Winds blow us to our permanent home, that we need no longer roam, but find that sanctuary where we can unpack and be a family.*

359

That You Can Put Your Kids Through College or Help Them at University if You Are Having a Tough Time Financially

Names of colleges you would like your kids to attend, in blue on white card ✳ Head and shoulder pictures of your children ✳ Glue ✳ A picture frame ✳ A shiny necklace for each child

TIMING

Thursday

360

THE SPELL

✳ Glue the children's pictures on the paper and frame the paper, saying, *Some day, your graduation certificates on the wall, and I will walk ten foot tall, if I can give you the key to a better world than your Mom/Dad and me, then that is all I want to see.*

✳ Hang the frame on the wall, loop the necklace/s over it, and say, *It may seem right now an impossibility, but I call the means for your fees to come to me, even miraculously.*

An All-Purpose Bariel, Angel
of Small Miracles Ritual

YOU WILL NEED

A large white candle * Nine small white candles surrounding it

TIMING

Any three consecutive days

THE SPELL

* Light the central candle and name what small miracle you need in your life, for whom, if not for you, and the ideal time frame.

* Now light each of the outer candle ring flames from the central one, saying, *Bariel, Angel of small miracles, this is the small miracle I do desire* [name it again] *and if granted I will do good in the world as a result of my bounty.*

* Blow out the small candles counterclockwise and then the large candle.

* Repeat the spell on two more days and on day 3 leave all the candles burning and use the accumulated energies to open yourself to infinite possibility.

An Egyptian Wealth Spell if You Love Beautiful Jewelry, Artifacts, or Gold but Can Never Afford to Own Any

A small piece of gold or tiny jewel set on a square of red velvet or silk ★ Three gold candles set in a triangle
★ A frankincense incense stick ★ Gold ribbon

TIMING

Sunday

THE SPELL

362

* Light the candles, the apex first, then hold the incense in each candle.

* In incense smoke, draw the Egyptian hieroglyph Collar of Gold over the gold/jewel and cloth. Say, *Gold/fine jewelry/lovely artifacts do I prize and would treasure them all, not value but beauty does me inspire, grant me Ancient Ones, to what I aspire.*

* When the candles are burned, roll the end of the cloth towards you and enclose the gold/jewel in the cloth. Secure the bundle with the ribbon.

* Keep it with anything precious that you have.

A Sekhmet, Lion Goddess of Ancient Egypt Ritual to Clear Your Debt Mountain and Make You Financially Secure

YOU WILL NEED

Ancient spell (bottom right) ✷ Seven obsidian arrows or flint arrowheads or any pointed crystals ✷ Red thread ✷ A red candle

I, Sekhmet, send forth these arrows against the misfortunes that have befallen me. May they aim true and return victorious that right order may be restored.

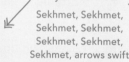

Sekhmet, Sekhmet, Sekhmet, Sekhmet, Sekhmet, Sekhmet, Sekhmet, arrows swift send out and swift return.

TIMING

Tuesday

THE SPELL

* Copy the ancient spell on white paper (or enlarge, scan, and print out)

* Put the spell paper flat on a table, with the seven arrows on top of the drawn ones.

* Light the candle behind it.

* Read or recite the spell, then roll the paper into a scroll with arrows tucked inside.

* Tie it with nine knots, saying, *May my debt mountain be bound, reduced, and removed by the power of Sekhmet and her fierce arrows, that I may know financial security, so I ask you protective Mother Lioness that it may be.*

* Let the candle burn.

* Keep the scroll with your financial documents.

About the Author

CASSANDRA EASON (Isle of Wight, England) is a best-selling author and a broadcaster on the paranormal. She has appeared many times on television and radio throughout the United States, Britain, Europe, and Australia. Cassandra originally trained as a teacher, and, while bringing up her five children, took a psychology honors degree with the intention of training as an educational psychologist.

A seemingly inexplicable psychic experience involving her two-year-old son Jack led to extensive research and the publication of a book on psychic children published by Random House in 1990. Since then, Cassandra has had more than 100 books published and translated into thirteen different languages. Cassandra also runs workshops in Australia and the United Kingdom and tours Australia each year. Many of her books have been serialized around the world and she has consulted with and contributed to such publications as the *UK Daily Mail, Daily Mirror, Daily Express, People, The Sun, News of the World* magazine, *Spirit and Destiny, Fate and Fortune, Prediction, Best and Bella, Homes and Gardens*, and *Good Housekeeping* and in *Woman's Day* and *New Idea* magazines in Australia. Cassandra now also regularly contributes to the UK magazine *Soul and Spirit*. She has long been acknowledged as a world expert on spellcraft and magick and has appeared many times on television and radio, including shows such as *Sky News*, ITV's *Strange but True*, BBC1's *Heaven and Earth*, and *Richard and Judy*, and she has also appeared in a series of mini films with Myleene Klass, and on Sky Living's *Jane Goldman Investigates*.